Jean—
I hope you enjoy
my book. I look
forward to your review—
let me know what you th

# Discovering
# Your True North

## Letters to Erin

*Randll*

Goose River Press
Waldoboro, Maine

Printed in United States of America

Library of Congress Card Number
2011932479

ISBN 978-1-59713-112-4
First Printing 2011

Published by:
Goose River Press
3400 Friendship Road
Waldoboro, Maine 04572

www.gooseriverpress.com

*To my girls:  Joann, Erin and Rae, without whom this would never have been written.  I will always love you.*

# CONTENTS

# CONTENTS (CONT.)

# ACKNOWLEDGEMENT

First and foremost, I'd like to thank my father, Henry Randall Thoms, and my late mother, Nanciellen Marie Dorler, for molding me into the man I am today.

Thank you Deborah Benner and Goose River Press. Deborah was a pleasure to work with. Her guidance and patience with this first time author made all the difference.

I'd also like to thank my editor, PJ Johnston, who was never shy about grammatical changes, but always preserved my thoughts and 'voice'.

And I don't know where I would be without my wife, Joann, and our daughter, Erin. I'm most grateful for their endless inspiration and unwavering patience and support that helped the dream of this book become a reality. Additionally, Joann's artistic talents and computer skills were invaluable in formatting the book and creating its cover design.

*"And do not go where the path may lead.
Go instead where there is no path
and leave a trail."*

*Ralph Waldo Emerson*

# THE SIX MISTAKES OF MAN

The Roman philosopher and orator, Cicero, unperturbed by the problems of politics which ultimately cost him his life, wrote these "Six Mistakes of Man'.

1 The delusion that individual gains and advancements are gained by crushing others.

2 The tendency to worry about things that cannot be changed or corrected.

3 Insisting a thing is impossible because we cannot accomplish it.

4 Refusing to set aside trivial references.

5 Neglecting development & refinement of the mind, and not acquiring the habit of reading & studying.

6 Attempting to compel others to believe and live as we do.

# INTRODUCTION
## SEPTEMBER 4, 2008

*Dear Erin,*
*Years ago, I had an idea for a book that would*
*offer my opinions on certain aspects of life that*
*can have a profound effect on one's individual de-*
*velopment and outlook. I began a feeble attempt*
*at writing it, but was not in the right frame of*
*mind to look at life objectively and/or philosophi-*
*cally. A confluence of recent events has made me*
*feel that now is the time to get my thoughts down*
*on paper...*

Next month your mom and I will be celebrating our fifteenth wedding anniversary. When we first met almost twenty years ago, I knew she was the one. Since then, my life has been nothing less than my dream come true. I think (almost daily) about how very lucky I am she took a chance on me. Together we're blessed to have you, one of the most special young ladies I've ever met.

Erin, you just started ninth grade at a new school. Even though you're very personable and outgoing, I know you're feeling somewhat uncomfortable in your new surroundings. Your mom and I try to support and understand you as you experience all that's 'new', but I'm certain the changes you're facing remain challenging.

Additionally, your sister has been dealing with tremendous personal challenges and change. It's been both upsetting and unnerving for your mom and I to watch her deal with so many difficult situations at once: graduating from college; breaking up with her longtime boyfriend; moving to a new place; starting a new job; getting mugged at gunpoint; and being involved in a terrible car accident that left her with serious burns, as well as a totaled vehicle. That list of things is beyond what most of us could ever hope to endure, yet your sister marches on. My hat's off to her for coping as well as she's been!

All of these events have made me a bit wistful, giving me a new sense of commitment to finish this book. I'm hoping to end up with something you'll read. Perhaps it will help you gain insight concerning the basis of your mother's and my concerns when we discuss certain issues with you.

Throughout the book I'll reference some of my past experiences in dealing with challenging issues and situations. I'll try to explain things as clearly as I can, while not dwelling on any of my personal emotional scars (yes, I do have them).

I want you to know I fully understand that growing up is difficult - especially adolescence. You haven't the wisdom yet to cope with many of the situations you'll encounter. In fact, it would be better not to have to experience some of what lies ahead.

Your environment, relationships and attitudes are in a constant state of flux. Sometimes the changes occur in the blink of an eye and sometimes at a more perceptible speed, but during adolescence everything is continually evolving. The thing to understand: it's all necessary for your personal development.

> . . . *You're not alone in your challenges and*
> *struggles. We all face them, and it's through*
> *them we discover our true north.*
> *Love,*
> *Dad*

# Chapter 1 Adolescence & Growing up-Parents & Peer Pressure

"Every youth owes it to himself and to the world to make the most possible out of the stuff that is in him..." Orison Swett Marden

*Dear Erin,*

*I want to talk with you more about growing up and the difficulties you'll experience, especially as a teenager. As you approach adulthood, life becomes more complex. Things will no longer simply be black or white. You'll start to discover endless nuances and innuendos - subtle shades of gray. It can become pretty difficult to find your path through it all. Parents and peer pressure will play the biggest roles, for better or worse, in your self-discovery. . .*

### DEALING WITH YOUR PARENTS

I've found the hardest part of growing up to be the mutable relationship between parent and child. When I use the term 'parent', of course I'm including stepparents.

A key thing to understanding parents in general is this: **we're not perfect**. We suffer from the same human flaws as you. (I never understood this fully until I was a parent myself.)

Your mother and I try to do what's best for you by teaching you what we believe is the right way for you to go about your life. That's our job. We aim to guide you down the right path, based on our knowledge and experience. Our parents (your grandparents) raised us in the same manner. We've all been raised or are being raised by role models who strongly influence us with their individual and subjective views and beliefs. But do you see the drawbacks to that? It can become very difficult for any of us as children, to look at things objectively so we can shape our own opinions and values.

When I was growing up, I had your grandfather to deal with - not an easy task. There were five of us, (me, your two uncles and two aunts) so, sometimes, it felt more like an army camp than a family. When your grandfather got especially exasperated with us he had a saying that he would use to put us in our place. He would say: "I may not always be right, but I'm never wrong". Even though that statement is a bit dictatorial and ridiculous, I do understand part of what he was trying to say.

More often than not, the things parents say are right, even though kids only choose to listen intermittently. Your mom and I may be wrong on occasion, but, as I've told you many times in the past, what we've learned has worked well enough for us both to get this far in life in one piece.

Erin, what we hope you gain from us is the best we have to offer - both as individuals and together as your parents. Sometimes it may be difficult to sort through what exactly our best is and what's purely 'parental noise', but it's vitally important for you to listen to it all and grasp our message to you. No matter how tedious and painful it may be, there's usually value in our words and actions.

We're on your side and only want what's best for you. It's important that you talk with us and we, in turn, listen to what you have to say. Please don't isolate yourself; don't ever be afraid to let us into your world. I know it can be difficult to hear opinions and receive answers that aren't to your liking (I have parents too), but remember we love you. Believe me when I say, I wish I'd paid more attention to what my parents were trying to tell me when I was a teenager. (So do they.)

## My Juvenile Delinquency

By now Erin, you may welcome a change in subject matter. Let me tell you a bit about my teenage years. There are some hard lessons I learned from experience and I'd like to keep you from doing the same.

Once upon a very long time ago, I was a carefree, fun-loving, naive, mostly irresponsible teenager, who periodically had very strained relationships with each of my parents. I say 'periodically' because it was (as so many things are) like the ebb and flow of the ocean tide. Sometimes I absolutely hated my parents; at other times, one or both of them were my friends.

My father (your grandfather) and I never really became close until I was in my late teens. My parents had separated and I guess it had more of an effect on me than I realized at the time. Initially, my mother (your grandmother) had custody of the five of us. I'm the oldest; I'm not sure whether that helped or hurt me.

By the time I was sixteen, I'd dropped out of high school. I'd begun hanging around with the wrong crowd and making bad decisions for myself. Thinking back, I was a know-it-all type of kid, who thought I was bulletproof; nothing could happen to me and no one was going to tell me what to do.

At some point during my derelict era, a friend of mine, Pete, stole his neighbor's car. I remember it being dark out and him stopping by to pick me up for a ride in this 'cherry' Chevy Impala.

Along the way, Pete asked if I wanted to drive. Heck yes! We pulled over, changed drivers and I started out. Within minutes, we were being chased by a police car. As it turned out, the owner of the stolen car had called them; they'd been actively looking for Pete and the car.

I found a place to pull over, shoved the car into park and we both ran off into the woods. The police found me right away. Pete turned himself in the next day.

Grandpa hadn't been around much since he and Grandma separated - until the minute I needed to be bailed out of jail. Unsure of what to do, Grandma must have called him. He came down to the jail to get me within a few hours. I was **truly** a scared puppy! Getting fingerprinted, having mug shots taken and spending a few hours locked up in the station holding cell all had a profound effect on this sixteen-year-old boy!

Dealing with the entire stolen car episode, Grandpa exemplified great parenting skills. The first thing we did was discuss what had happened over breakfast. Wow!! Grandpa didn't freak out! He treated me like a young man instead of a punk kid who didn't know his ass from his elbow.

My memory may be a little fuzzy concerning some of the details, but I believe we had a meeting with the lawyer he'd retained for me after our breakfast. Later, we went to Schwartz's, one of the nicest men's clothing stores in town at the time. Grandpa bought me a new suit so I'd make a good impression in court. **AND**, by the end of the day I was signed back into high school, after a meeting Grandpa had arranged for the two of us with the high school principal.

Erin, I couldn't believe how systematically and orderly Grandpa had started me on my personal road to recovery. He'd been there for me when I needed him most and set my life back on a positive track. I hate to think where I would have ended up had he not taken the actions he did, or handled the situation in the manner he had.

Historically, Grandma has always been in my corner. She's helped me to look more closely at myself and my situation and to view things more positively. Her well-explained lessons have always been delivered in a very deliberate and patient manner. Listening to 'the why' part of each lesson was a tremendous help for me in understanding many of the situations I found myself in while growing up. Grandma's parenting style made it much easier to discuss virtually any subject with her, garnering her my trust and respect, but Erin, if you go back to the

Discovering Your True North

beginning of this chapter you'll read that there were times I hated her anyway. Why? I was a hormonal, temperamental and moody teenager who thought he knew it all. I wanted things to go my way, always. Sound familiar?

I like to think some of your grandparents' traits have rubbed off on me. I feel I'm a blend of the best they each have to offer. It was their love, care and perseverance that kept me from pissing away my potential and helped mold me into a more loving, caring, understanding and responsible man- maybe even a pretty great dad!

## PEER PRESSURE

Erin, by now I'm quite sure you're familiar with peer pressure. It can be overwhelming during adolescence because of the feelings of insecurity and uncertainty you may have. These feelings are magnified by not yet understanding your place in life, or what your true abilities are.

Peer pressure comes in all shapes and sizes, doesn't it? It has a tremendous hold over all of us as kids because the need to fit in, be accepted and belong is so overpowering. Kids also need to feel loved (although as a teen, I'm not sure it's possible to fully comprehend the concept).

As parents, your mom and I are always going to be concerned about to whom and what you want to belong. That's part of our job, so please respect our curiosity in wondering exactly what you're doing, when and with whom.

I mentioned my run-in with the law earlier. The (peer) pressure I encountered to be a part of Pete's world seemed overwhelming at the time. I **needed** to belong. If I didn't see things the way he and his friends did, I'd become an outcast.

Erin, in spite of the risk of becoming an outcast or labeled 'not cool', sometimes it's crucial to resist the peer pressure you experience. There's nothing wrong with just saying 'no' if something doesn't feel right to you. Always listen to your gut; it'll never lie.

Your teenage friends don't have the answers anymore than you do. They think they know it all, but they're trying to find their own way like you are. Just because they throw themselves off a cliff doesn't mean you need to follow.

Let me give you a personal example. While I was exposed to it repeatedly growing up, there was one area of peer pressure I never gave in to: drugs.

I grew up at the tail end of the 'Woodstock' era. Most of my friends were using drugs of all kinds. Understand, it was a period of open rebellion against long established social norms, therefore almost any aspect of the establishment was an acceptable target of protest by the younger generation.

While I always drank beer and smoked cigarettes back then, drug use was not acceptable to me. I never even had the desire to inhale marijuana. But a funny thing happened - my friends eventually stopped pressuring me and accepted that I couldn't be swayed from my position. This may have been the first step of me becoming my own person.

With the passage of time, I've seen many friends end up in jail with ruined lives; and many die way too soon, all because of drugs – including my friend, Pete.

Here's something you'll eventually discover: many of the 'cool' kids in high school will end up becoming shallow, troubled adults. These childhood idols tend to be among the most lost of all of us. The reason they work extra hard at trying to be the coolest and getting all of us to go along with them, is simply so they, themselves, will fit in somewhere. Instead of trying to fit in with them, work on being comfortable in your own skin and going your own way.

There's a secret nobody tells you: in high school, everything hinges upon fitting in. From the day you graduate and enter the real world, everything hinges upon standing out. The most successful people figure this out early on.

### SEX AND SEXUALITY

Beyond the ever constant presence of drugs and pressure to use them, you and your friends will be consistently challenged by the number one issue on every teenage mind: sex and sexuality.

All the changes taking place during adolescence make it impossible to get away from the discussion and potential involvement in sexual activity. Teenagers will be made to feel like real oddballs if they don't experience it (peer pressure, once again).

The potential consequences of sexual activity have been discussed ad nauseum. Nonetheless, Erin, I feel the need to give you my honest, unbridled opinion concerning sex and how it can be damaging during your formative years - especially being a teenage girl.

For adolescent girls, there comes a growing need to nurture, as well as to feel loved, cared for and understood. As I mentioned earlier, I don't think any teen really understands the concept of love; teenage girls seem to be more vulnerable because of these misconceptions. When you package youthful misinterpretations (about love), with raging hormones and add a little 'nothing bad will happen to me' attitude, you lay the groundwork for personal sorrow and tragedy. Your mom and I want to save you from this.

One would hope in today's world that all teens are aware of the dangers of unprotected sex: unwanted pregnancy, sexually transmitted diseases (STD's) and AIDS, but there are other troubling consequences.

I remember some of the more promiscuous girls in high school and the reputations they earned. Talk about peer pressure and its negative impact on a person! Being labeled as 'sluts' and continually talked about behind their backs did nothing to help build their self-esteem, or make them feel more 'womanly'. Many of these girls never recovered from their disastrous adolescent sexual experiences. They continue to bear the emotional scars today, as evidenced by the nature of their adult relationships.

Call it righteous retribution, but some of the people paying for the way they contributed to the dysfunctional development of these girls are the boys with whom they were involved. Many wound up in unhappy relationships with these girls as their wives and girlfriends. More than a few wound up as accidental co-parents.

Erin, it's important that you fully understand the psyche of **ALL** teenage boys. Teenage boys have one thing on their minds all day, every day. They want to have sex and will say and do anything in order to accomplish this. And don't be fooled! **ANY** female with a pulse will do. Let me repeat that another way: Teenage boys will tell a girl whatever she wants to hear, and do whatever she asks, so long as the prize is her sexual submission. It's **never** complimentary when a young man wants to have sex with you; if you decline the ride, it's no problem for him! Another bus will be along in 20 minutes. Promise me you'll never forget that.

That sounds harsh, you say? I was once one of those boys and that type of behavior is typical for a teenage male, ruled by hormones. Some call this a 'rite of passage'. Society even contributes to its acceptability by brushing it off and saying, 'Boys will be boys'.

There will be teenage girls out there who think their boyfriends aren't like that at all. ('He's loving and caring'. 'He would never do anything to hurt me'.) This is simply not the case. It will be many years before a teenage boy can think about **any** relationship in terms other then sexual.

Of course, teenage boys can be negatively impacted by their sexual interaction growing up too. The way they treat girls shapes how they interact with women later in life. Some grown men continue to think of women as nothing more than conquests, or 'pieces of meat', either consciously or sub-consciously. This attitude is deemed acceptable by society - remember, 'Boys will be boys'!

Last night I was watching a popular sitcom on TV where one of the main characters is a happy-go-lucky bachelor. His basic make-up is that of a womanizer, yet he's made out to be a **great guy**. Some of the other characters on the show even express feeling a bit sorry for him. Erin, exactly how does womanizing behavior constitute being a 'great guy'?

. . . *in summary, the entire process of growing up is a constant series of trials and tribulations you'll need to face and conquer. You can't run and hide from them. Whenever an opportunity arises, seize it. Be sure to learn what the pitfalls are so you can avoid them.*

*Once you successfully overcome the challenges you'll encounter, your reward will be more of life's adventures. You get to move to the next level and face further tests of your mettle. Erin, always leave yourself open to accepting these ever bigger challenges, pushing the envelope of excellence.*

*Love,*

*Dad*

## CHAPTER 2   FAMILY

"A family is a place where minds come in contact with one another."  Buddha

*Dear Erin,*
*I've already touched on the subject of family by discussing the dynamics of the relationship you can expect to have with your parents, but families are more complex than just a parent-child relationship.   Most families consist of many individuals as diverse as the colors in a spectrum of light.   It can make for very interesting interactions and situations. . .*

## WHAT IS FAMILY?

Of course, there are two types of family: nuclear and extended. Most people, you included, are lucky enough to have both.

Your extended family tends to have far less effect on your daily life, while your nuclear family exercises tremendous influence over you and your development. In your case, this is your mom and me, along with your sister Rae.

Look around our home, Erin. Our family may be a group of people to whom you might not ever have gotten close given a different set of circumstances; however, we're the ones on the front line with you at your best and worst. We're the ones who live with the aftermath of **ALL** your actions, be they messes or successes. We're the people least likely to have ulterior motives for what we ask and expect of you.

What does that matter? Your mom and I hope it provides you with comfort and security. We want you to have an environment that will allow you to drop your defenses and be yourself. I hope it enables you to speak freely with us about any subject, as well as to listen to what we may have to say. Two-way exchanges with us, based on trust and respect, will help you learn a great deal about yourself. And, no, it won't always be to your liking. Some of your most important lessons are bound to be gift wrapped in some really ugly paper!

## YOUR PERSONAL SAFETY NET

Erin, I mentioned families being on the front line with you, in good times and bad. I've experienced these types of situations and would like to share one or two examples with you.

I was married before I married your mother (when I was far too young), to someone I dated in high school. Our relationship was tumultuous at best: an infatuation-driven roller coaster ride, riddled with immaturity, infidelity and financial irresponsibility, peppered with verbal and physical abuse. There was no love; neither of us truly cared about the other. Our marriage ended abruptly when I simply couldn't stand it any longer and I told her to have her parents come and get her; I never wanted to see her again.

The first few weeks we were separated were quite an eye opener! Bills I'd known nothing about began rolling in and I was **shocked** to see many were in arrears! Without my knowledge, I'd become a credit liability. As a friend of mine once told me, 'If it cost a quarter to go around the world you couldn't afford to get out of sight'.

Overwhelmed? Scared? Not sure of what to do? **You bet**! So, you know where I started, Erin? I called your Grandpa and asked for his advice. He told me "First, give it some more time so you can determine the scope of the damage"

Within short order, it became obvious I was in a tremendous financial jam, **way** over my head! I owed north of thirteen thousand dollars (all debt that was past due) with **absolutely nothing** to show for it! (Remember, I'm referring to the 1970's. This figure would translate into much more in today's economy.) There was no way I'd be able to support myself in the short term with such debt.

Grandpa pulled me from the brink of financial ruin. Not only did he allow me to move home so I could dedicate **all** of my limited resources to getting out of debt; he even made payments for me on several occasions, when I was threatened with wage garnishment and other legal action. His only caveat?  That no one knew about it. (I've never mentioned it until now.)

Another example of my personal family safety net in action involved your Grandma.  I told you earlier I'd always felt comfortable discussing my most personal issues with her; I did just that when I first met your mom, Erin.

When your mom and I first became acquainted, we were both in the midst of lousy relationships:  I was living with someone and your mom was unhappily married.  I knew early on that your mom was the one for me; I just didn't know if anything would ever come of it.  There were so many obstacles!

On numerous occasions, Grandma listened to me pour my heart out to her about my feelings for your mom. She helped me keep myself together, mentally and emotionally, while I waited to see if your mom and I would become a couple.  I can't begin to tell you how much that meant to me!

You'll find, as most of us do, that you'll receive such assistance, as well as return it in kind.  After all, everyone experiences times when life slaps them in the face and they need a hand to get back up on their feet again.  The universe works in balance, Erin.  It's all about give **AND** take.

## YOUR FAMILY'S NEEDS

What about the times your family wants too much from you?

At one time or another, you're bound to be swamped at work, up to your armpits with your personal life, and what they want, or need, becomes too much of a strain on you. I don't care who you are, Erin, it's going to happen! My best advice is to weigh each situation **very** carefully. Prioritize. Ideally, no one's needs should ever end up damaging you, your health or your personal life. What good would you be to anyone if you allowed that to happen?

And there will be those times you'll have to refrain from getting involved in a family member's plight solely because they're not making any personal effort to better their own situation. Otherwise you'll become nothing more than an 'enabler', perpetuating unhealthy behavior in that needy person. I'm a firm believer in the adage 'the Lord helps those who help themselves'.

It's hard to understand why some people are motivated and others aren't; why some people bitch and moan and other's don't; why some people have big gray clouds of negativity around them and others are like rays of sunshine. All these different types of people will be present in your family – nuclear and extended - and it won't be difficult at all to identify which family members are which. The members that everyone wants to spend time around will be the positive, productive ones.

## SURROGATE FAMILIES

Erin, we all know or know of people who are orphaned or estranged You may be thinking, "Where does all this leave them?"

Families aren't necessarily made up of blood relatives. There can be, and often are, friends who become as close as, or closer than, siblings, parents or grandparents – to name just a few examples. These surrogates need to be proven trustworthy, of course, and trust can only be earned over time.

The only way to get through life without any kind of personal support network is through personal choice. Why would someone want to? I don't know, but you'll meet people who've chosen that path. Talk about creating a lonely, empty, unhappy life for oneself! Take any problem, add 'isolation' and you can wind up with anything from clinical depression to suicide.

> . . . *You should always appreciate your family;*
> *never take them for granted. When all else fails,*
> *their unconditional love and support will be*
> *what carries you through.*
> *Love,*
> *Dad*

## Chapter 3   Friendship

"A friend is one that knows you as you are, understands where you have been, accepts what you have become, and still, gently allows you to grow."
William Shakespeare

*Dear Erin,*
*I think it's important to discuss friends and friendship. The affect people close to you can have on your wellbeing and development can't be overstated. It can make or break you. There's an old saying, 'You are the company you keep'. It's so true. Try to remember that when deciding who is, and who may not be, your friend. . .*

Friendship comes in all different varieties. There are 'fair weather' friends, work friends, environmental friends and true friends, to name a few. I've even made several phone friends of the vendors I deal with at work on a regular basis.

Erin, I'm sure by now you know what a 'fair weather' friend is and probably have several of them. These are the people who are with you as long as they're having fun and it doesn't require too much effort or emotional involvement on their part. As a rule, these are not the kind of friends you can rely on or trust in when the chips are down. The minute things between you and them get too complicated or personal, they'll become distant or disappear from your view altogether.

Work friends are very similar to 'fair weather' friends, but they share your place of employment. While it's beneficial to be liked by your colleagues, always remember what competition in the workplace does to people. These 'friends' will most assuredly be looking out for their own interests; not concerned, in any way, about yours. The workplace is often where you'll see people perfect the art of backstabbing.

Then we have one of my favorites - environmental friends. They're in a class all by themselves because of the profound effect they can have on you as a person. It can be positive or negative, depending on the 'environment' in question. Because you mean so much to me, I'll always be concerned about which environments you choose for yourself.

Let me give you a good and bad example of how environmental friends can influence and reinforce your behavior.

Years ago, I was a chain smoker. One of the reasons I have respiratory issues today (asthma, pneumonia, etc.) is years of inhaling the smoke of the mentholated Salem cigarettes I loved.

Because of this utterly idiotic and life-threatening habit, I found myself surrounded by a whole group of like-minded, smoking friends. Some of them were truly great people in other respects, but they did nothing to help my habit. After several years of stupidity and ignorance, I finally figured out, if I really wanted to stop smoking, I had to change my environment.

Within short order, after I quit smoking, my entire circle of smoking friends disappeared right along with the habit. Although I hated to see some of these people vanish from my life, it was far more important that I remove myself from the unhealthy atmosphere and not worry about who would remain afterwards. Erin, there will be times when it will be in your best interests to make similar choices.

The other side of having environmental friends is the pleasant and positive affect they may bring with them. Such was the case with Grandpa and his weekend pilot buddies.

When I was growing up, Grandpa was extensively involved in piloting small, single engine aircraft. He was obsessed enough with flying that he got a part-time job, solely to support his passion. He flew almost exclusively out of three local airports: Sky Acres in LaGrangeville, N.Y.; Kobelt Airport in Wallkill, N.Y.; and Stormville Airport in Hopewell Junction, N.Y. You could find him at one of these hangouts virtually every weekend.

Many weekends when Grandpa went flying, I got to tag along. Weather permitting, we flew planes such as: Cessna 140s; 150s; and, my favorite, the J-3 Piper Cub. You can do a search online to see what these were like. To this day I remember fondly the time I spent in the front seat of a J-3 flying with Grandpa (this particular plane is flown from the back seat). What ended up being the most enjoyable part of this time we spent together, though, was hanging out with all of his pilot friends.

It turns out there were many 'weekend warriors' just as obsessed with flying as Grandpa was. Being the social person he was, he had many piloting friends. Among these men, there was always a healthy dose of regular guy talk, interspersed with informative conversations about how to improve one's flying skills. Some of the piloting tips discussed included: how to decipher the current weather map; how the newest radio equipment worked; or even how to make better use of the flight instrument panel. Although he doesn't fly anymore, Grandpa maintains several of his pilot friendships today, more than 40 years later.

Erin, there will be times and situations where it will not immediately be evident who may fit into which category of friend. You may feel like a particular relationship is more than it really is. You might even start investing a lot of time trying to make it grow. Regardless, it takes two to tango. Unless both parties want a friendship to evolve, it won't.

While we're discussing how friendships can evolve, I want to share my thoughts on something called 'friends with benefits'. This unique dynamic between people seems far more prevalent in today's world than twenty-five or thirty years ago. The world in which you're growing up is far more liberal, with less emphasis on traditional committed relationships.

Please be aware of the emotional pitfalls this kind of relationship can bring with it and why I'd urge you not to get involved in it.

Years ago, when I was an energetic, single, twenty-five year old, I met Patti. She and her husband of many years were in business together in the mall where I worked. They had a couple kids and seemed to be living a pretty typical, middle class, married life. I found her to be engaging, fun loving and easy to talk to. She was the first older woman with whom I genuinely enjoyed spending time and to whom I really connected. The feeling was mutual and we became very good friends.

Patti's husband always seemed a bit odd to me. He had an effeminate air that I couldn't quite put my finger on. It turned out Patti had been noticing it as well, for quite some time.

One day over coffee, with tears in her eyes, Patti told me her husband had 'come out of the closet' and admitted to her he was gay. He'd only been managing to keep up the happily married façade (for as long as he had) for the sake of their kids. He felt he could no longer deny his true desires.

Patti was devastated by her husband's confession. Not only had he felt this way for a long time, he'd even had sexual encounters with men. She found herself feeling very alone, her femininity shattered. She needed a friend in whom she could confide and on whom she could lean.

I was more then willing and eager to spend time with her doing whatever she wanted.

My relationship with Patti grew closer as the weeks and months went on, albeit limited by her marital and familial obligations. In the beginning, we had a wonderful time whenever we were together. She needed the energy and fun I offered, while I was experiencing many new and exciting things being with an older woman. However, once our relationship became sexual, the idyllic picture changed.

The emotions involved in my 'friends with benefits' arrangement with Patti became confusing and upsetting in short order. I ended up playing a role in a part-time intimate relationship without the commitment you'd normally expect to have.

Some people may think having a part-time, casual, sexual relationship with someone would be a great thing - like having your cake and eating it too. I found the part-time nature of such a relationship brought with it many difficult and unpleasant emotional issues.

I felt enormous amounts of jealousy, mistrust and hurt. The fun vanished as my feelings of despair became overwhelming. I began to question myself and why I was involved in such a mess. How had I let it happen? I wondered what her time with him was like. Would I see her again? When? Should I end it? How? I was literally driving myself crazy.

The end of my relationship with Patti came after an evening we'd spent together at my place. The next morning as I was having coffee trying to face the new day, the doorbell rang. I went downstairs and Patti's husband was standing there. I didn't know what to think. He knew we'd been spending time together and hadn't had any objections to that point. Erin, I can't begin to tell you how uncomfortable I was when I opened the door.

Patti had sent him by to fetch her wedding ring which she had left in my apartment! Talk about a mind blower of an experience! He was acting very nonchalant about the whole situation, so I played along. I got the ring, gave it to him and he went on his merry way as if nothing had happened. Erin, think about how you'd react to something like that!

I realized, then and there, the ramifications of this relationship were far more than I'd bargained for; it had to end. Later that day, I had a heart to heart with Patti and told her of my decision. Even though she was surprised and upset by my bowing out, she understood why I needed to take a step back from us.

Erin, I'd urge you not to ever get caught up in a 'friends with benefits' situation, regardless of how innocent and carefree it may seem. It's too difficult to maintain a status quo of non-commitment in any intimate relationship for things to work out well.

I'd like to make another point very clear concerning getting close to anyone new. At some point, you'll need to decide if they're a potential danger to you, or not. If you feel they could be, please don't go out of your way trying to attract their attention. If you have any doubts about someone with respect to this, you're better off just walking away. Remember, trust your gut.

Determining if a person is worthy of your friendship, or not, may be as easy as establishing a personal checklist of things that are taboo for you. One of the no-nos for me is drug use of any kind. Anyone who would bring a negative like that into a relationship is not worth my time or energy.

Erin, trying to cultivate certain friendships can be very frustrating. You meet someone you really like and decide to try to get closer to them; maybe you even start getting a little possessive and/or emotionally attached. No matter what you do, certain relationships just never seem to gain any traction. Depending on what your level of involvement and attachment, having someone 'spurn your advances' can be devastating.

Rejection is one of the hardest things for us all to deal with. You naturally want to be liked and accepted by your friends and family. When it doesn't go according to plan, you can end up feeling very vulnerable and maybe even worthless. Don't be too hard on yourself when a friendship is over.

Through the course of your life, new friends will come into view and others will fade out, over and over again. Sometimes a friendship that seemed to have faded out completely may re-emerge. Only on rare occasions will you be able to successfully cultivate what I call a true friendship.

A true friend is an especially rare commodity in today's fast paced world. Seldom will you meet someone you genuinely enjoy being around who enjoys your company equally in return. It becomes even more amazing when the two of you always seem able to make time for each other.

A true friend is someone who will always be there for you, in whatever capacity needed, whenever you ask. You'll have no problem doing the same in return. You don't ask why because you never feel taken for granted, or used in any way. You simply enjoy being in this person's company, no matter the circumstance.

Erin, you know my friend Vanessa is one of those people with whom I genuinely enjoy spending time, no matter what we're doing. There was just something that clicked for us when we first met almost twenty-five years ago.

My friendship with Vanessa has flourished over the years in spite of our ever-changing circumstances. At different times, we've worked together and seen each other part of every workday. In fact, we've worked together at three different companies over the years. Then there are other periods of time where we won't see or hear from each other for several months. Regardless of the amount of contact we have, she will always be one of my closest friends. We've shared many personal things with each other, cried on each others' shoulders and laughed our butts off together.

If you have true friends like Vanessa, you know there's an inexplicable bond. This bond is further reinforced by years of emotional and personal 'deposits' made into your joint friendship account.

In the case of Vanessa, I know I annoy her quite often. She may even annoy me once in awhile, although I can't remember the last time she did. In spite of any differences we have, we always like and respect each other. If sticking points cause us to have any kind of difficult moment at all, it's quickly forgotten. It's easy to forgive and forget when someone's special to you.

Erin, it's important to remember to make the emotional and personal deposits as part of a friendship. Sometimes the most insignificant thing can have everlasting effects and cement a relationship.

My friend Mike would be a great example of a solid friendship. Sometimes several years will go by without us seeing, or even hearing from each other, but when we get together, the conversation easily picks up where it left off, as if we just saw each other yesterday.

One evening after not seeing or hearing from Mike for two or three years, he called me from Florida. He'd recently relocated to get a new start for himself. He was working in his parent's breakfast restaurant as a short order cook during the week. In order to make some extra money, he'd started tending bar on the weekends. A friend of his recruited him to work at a local redneck gin mill bordering an Indian reservation near Lake Okeechobee (you can't make something like this up).

Mike is a fantastic bartender. He has an almost magical way of getting along with the customers while still maintaining a semblance of law and order. This bar was evidently an exceptionally wild place. A volatile mix of people hung out there. There was more than a fair amount of firearms and drugs to go along with the already highly alcohol-charged atmosphere. Mike was just the man for the job; you see, he was quite the wild man himself.

As was told to me, the environment in the bar was a bit racially charged. The local Indian girls had this game they liked to play where they would try to lure unsuspecting white guys into a compromising situation. Of course, the local Indian men hated the whole idea of this and would often get a hold of these 'innocents', beating the hell out of them, or worse. I was told there were occasional murders because of these interracial trysts. There was never a dull moment according to Mike, who kept a length of pipe at the ready behind the bar. "You never know when I may need to get in the middle of something", he told me. He was bartender and bouncer all in one and had to be alert every second.

For whatever reason, on this particular night Mike felt like he needed to talk to a real friend. Someone he could open up to and who would be supportive (he absolutely hated being lectured to about anything he did). He was having an exceptionally difficult evening maintaining control. He needed a momentary respite to get his mind off of what was going on. Something made him think to call me.

Mike said he wanted to find out what I'd been up to. The reality was he needed me to make him laugh a little and help him regain his sanity. He was half in the bag from all the drinks some of his new 'friends' had been buying him throughout the evening. I'm not sure if he would remember having this conversation with me or not. We talked for more than half an hour. It was a huge mutual deposit into our friendship account.

Erin, one thing I've learned about getting along with people, especially your friends, is you must accept they're human beings. Everybody has their own little quirks, some of which will be quite aggravating to you. You invariably have qualities that will bother other people just as much. It's all a part of the human condition.

If you hope to be friendly with anyone, you'll need to accept some of their personal foibles as part of the deal. Always try to remember, as far as basic personalities go, a leopard never changes spots. This means if you think you can drastically change a person's make up so they'll better mesh with you somehow - forget it. Friend or lover, it makes no difference.

Part of accepting a person at face value will be your ability to be sympathetic to and empathetic with them. You'll need to be able to relate to them on their level, seeing things from their vantage point. That will require a certain understanding of the type of personality with which you're dealing. For example, if a particular friend is sensitive, you'll need to speak with them in a certain manner and tone. A more gregarious personality (a Type A person, for example) would be dealt with in a completely different manner. I don't know if this is really as hard as it sounds. There's an organic quality to friendship that makes conversation flow fairly easily.

Friendship requires patience, understanding and empathy. It also requires a touch of open-mindedness and acceptance. The more open-minded you are, the wider your circle of friends will be.

*. . . If you're lucky, you'll end up having many friendships throughout your life. Some of these will be of the closest and most personal nature. Others will be nothing more than casual acquaintances. All will help in rounding out your personality by helping you see things about yourself and the world you may have missed otherwise.*
*Love,*
*Dad*

# CHAPTER 4 HONESTY, LOYALTY AND TRUST

"Honesty is the first chapter of the book of wisdom." Thomas Jefferson

*Dear Erin,*
*I want to talk with you about three traits you'll rarely find in people; for me they're also the most admirable and treasured: honesty, loyalty and trust. I've met very few in my life with these characteristics. I hope, after reading this, you'll decide to embrace them as your own. . . .*

## HONESTY

Honesty seems a straightforward enough concept that shouldn't require any additional elaboration. We've all had our parents drum into us that 'Honesty is the best policy', but are we truly honest?

There may be times when you think it's okay to tell a white lie so as not to hurt someone you care about. On occasion, it may seem easier to embellish the truth and spare yourself an uncomfortable moment. I'm not referring to this level of dishonesty. (Don't get me wrong – I'd like to think, beyond a shadow of a doubt, that you'd always tell the truth.). I venture to say we've all found ourselves in situations where a fib here and there can make life more fluid and pleasant.

What I look for and admire in others, is hearing the unvarnished truth, no matter what. Truly honest people can be relied on to tell it like it is. At times it can be extremely tough and uncomfortable to do, but in the long run you'll be better off telling the truth - **always**. Someone who can be direct, even when they know they may be compromising themselves in the process, is someone I want by my side.

Erin, it's only natural, when you feel threatened, to want to protect yourself. Your instinctive response may be to lie. I've been guilty of this myself, on occasion, in the past. However, I don't ever recall being dishonest when it really mattered. I've taken my medicine **many times** - even when it's caused me great personal injury - because I wasn't willing to lie. Let me tell you about one such instance where the truth caused me great pain, before you were even a twinkle in my eye.

I was involved with a woman who shall remain name-less. We'd been living together comfortably for a few years, but the relationship was completely stagnant for most of that time. We had no future plans together and never dis-cussed anything other than what we were doing in the mo-ment. There was absolutely nothing to look forward to other then the apparent security we felt being together.

Looking back now, I believe she had low self-esteem and it was impossible for her to truly love anyone. She was as secretive and protective of her thoughts and de-sires as she was of her past and didn't ever seem truly happy. It was as if she was only going through the mo-tions of living, as I was when I met her. Initially, that was our common bond.

While this live-in relationship of mine was approach-ing a critical juncture for me, out of nowhere I suddenly had another young lady working very hard to get my at-tention. This new female friend was a fresh face and I very much needed something different and exciting in my life. She was fun to be with, easy to talk to and not demand-ing of me in anyway. We liked each other and started spending more time together, albeit platonically.

My new best 'gal friend' was making me see things about my live-in relationship I'd been blind to for quite some time. The light-hearted air she brought with her showed me what had been lacking with my live-in. She thought I should strive to have more than just a habit to go home to. All of what she brought to my life was very gratifying. I slowly felt myself drifting away from home.

This new friendship/relationship progressed nicely until one night when I was at my new gal pal's condo. As we were drinking a glass of wine and discussing our personal 'woes du jour', one thing led to another.

I'm not sure if you've ever seen the movie "When Harry met Sally". If you have, you'll remember them discussing friendship between a man and a woman. Harry believed there was always a certain level of sexual tension that existed between a man and a woman. Well, there was definitely that element of tension in the air that evening.

Erin, after my infidelity, a tsunami of guilt completely overwhelmed me! I started asking myself all kinds of questions. I didn't know how or why I'd ended up in that position. How could I have done something so underhanded? How could I have been such an ass? I felt **unbelievably** horrible!

I ended up leveling with my live-in about my indiscretion. It was one of the hardest things I'd ever had to admit to, but I did, nonetheless. The truth proved to be very traumatic for her. In fact, her emotional reaction was far greater than any I'd ever seen from her for any reason. She felt tremendously hurt and betrayed, lashing out at me for the next several days.

Needless to say my live-in and I went our separate ways. It turned out she'd been looking for a reason to end it between us for quite some time. This episode was just what the doctor ordered to give her enough gumption. While I don't condone any of what happened, remarkably it ended up being the best thing for both of us.

Honey, in this one instance your dear old dad had violated two of the three traits I treasure most in people. I'd deeply hurt someone who loved and trusted me. She'd believed I would be loyal and faithful to her no matter what and I hadn't been. But in spite of all the pain I knew it would cause, I still told the truth.

This episode of my life taught me you can't pick and choose which of the three tenets (honesty, trust and loyalty) you live by or when you live by them. They come together as a package deal and you need to make the commitment to all three together. I'm proud to say I have.

The temptation when confronted with uncomfortable situations to be dishonest, or stretch the truth, may seem irresistible. Why take the road less traveled and suffer for it? Just embellish a little so things run smoothly and everything will end up fine, right?

The problem is things often don't end up fine when deception's part of the equation. There's a reason 'Honesty is the best policy'. It hurts when we're lied to about anything.

You'll meet some people who choose to live their lives lying to the extreme in an effort to endlessly promote themselves above all else. It can get to the point where they're forever weaving wonderful tales for all to hear. The challenge for them then becomes remembering what they told to whom. Ultimately, this is their downfall. You'll be able to pick them out of the crowd. Stay away from people who live their lives in this manner. They'll throw you under the bus if that's what's needed to better their position.

From my observation of liars over the years, lying's just too much work. If you're in a situation where it's too difficult to tell the truth, say nothing.

At times when I've been put in an awkward position, I've not always answered someone directly, if at all. I may even try to change the subject or respond in such a way as to change the entire direction of the conversation. But I won't lie.

Even if you have to respond by saying, "I'd rather not answer that question", in the long run you'll be better off. You don't ever want to end up with the reputation of being a liar.

## LOYALTY

Loyalty is another rare quality I admire in people. Over the years, I've witnessed remarkably few instances of it. I think it's because there's an inherent 'covering your ass' mentality built-in to all of us. Don't get me wrong, sweetheart, looking out for number one should always be first and foremost. But what if you're in a situation where someone, or some cause genuinely worthwhile, needs your support? What if a person you truly care about is being used as the sacrificial lamb even though they don't deserve being put in that position? I experienced just such a situation first hand when I worked as the manager of a shoe store in Watertown, VT.

I'd worked for a reasonably large shoe company for a couple years when I was promoted to manager. I was assigned a brand new store in a newly constructed strip mall in Watertown, VT. and given the responsibility of getting the new store ready to open for business. This included the hiring and training of my staff, except for the assistant manager.

The assistant manager assigned to me was specially chosen and transferred in from another store to work with me. It was considered a promotion for him. However, the underlying reason was so he could learn from me. The company wanted me to straighten him out, or they were going to cut him loose. Everyone had high hopes this change of scenery would spark change within him.

It turned out my assistant manager was a very troubled individual. He had many personal issues including a precarious financial situation. I was alerted by my staff to keep an eye on him. They didn't think he could be trusted; neither did I.

Because of the minimum number of man-hours we were using to run the store, it was difficult to watch over anyone not pulling their own weight. We all did our best, but in this atmosphere, a certain level of trust was essential. We had to be a team and work together or the store couldn't function properly within budgeted payroll limits.

After the store had been open for about a year, I was subjected to my first audit. Audits were called at random by the company to make sure things were as they should be. For any of the company's store managers, the mere thought of an audit was worrisome. You want to believe everything's perfect, but an audit was the litmus test, proof for all to see. You can't hide anything from a good auditor.

Sometime during the second day, it was obvious I had shrinkage in my inventory, about a thousand dollars worth. Looking at it in terms of the short staffing we were forced to operate within; having better then $250,000.00 in inventory to watch over, a thousand dollar shortage was not really excessive. But no one could understand it, so fingers started pointing. Most of them pointed in the direction of my assistant manager.

Without knowing it, in separate interviews with both the district manager and auditor, my staff and I were all in agreement. If our inventory was off, my assistant manager was the thief. We suspected he'd been fooling around with refunds given on fictitious returns, in order to help his personal cash flow problem.

What made my audit more difficult than normal was the somewhat contentious past I'd had with my district manager. Regardless of how good a job I was doing, he'd wanted me out of the picture for quite some time. I had many other allies within the company, so up until audit time he hadn't been able to do anything about that 'pain in the ass out in Watertown' (me).

My regional manager (the DM's boss), along with all three managers I'd worked for prior to my promotion, thought I walked on water. With my mediocre audit results now to back him, my district manager finally had the ammunition he needed to terminate me. He was in for a surprise!

My staff at the shoe store loved me. As their manager I wasn't an easy taskmaster, but I was always fair with them. I treated them like human beings and liked them all. We had a real feeling of camaraderie and mutual respect not often experienced in the workplace.

When my termination appeared imminent, I decided to resign. I offered no resistance, no defense, nor voiced any reason for my last minute decision. I was simply tired of all the company politics and dealing with a district manager who'd been working so hard against my success. I knew it was a no-win situation. I realized if I were to somehow survive this attack, it would never get any better for me. Plus, quite honestly, **it always feels better being the 'dumper' instead of the 'dumpee.'** I was able to walk away with my head held high.

Upon being told I'd stepped down as manager, my staff was in shock. They couldn't believe I was being railroaded out of the company while the guy responsible for the poor audit was retained. They expressed their displeasure, but were simply ignored. Realizing how futile it was to try and defend me, they each immediately resigned. They all told the district manager there was no way they could work for such an ignorant and uncaring company. They had no doubt I was trustworthy. How could they (the company) have treated me like they had? What would keep the same thing from happening to them in the future? Even after they were all offered substantial raises to stay (some of them had been long overdue), not a single one of them even blinked. We'd worked together as a team and now walked out as one.

Erin, you may think this display of loyalty to be insignificant. For me it was an act of allegiance I hadn't ever experienced before. It was, and still is, a big deal for me personally. To have one highly valued full-time and three part-time people up and quit in unison, because of how I'd been treated, was very humbling.

Please understand, I don't think people should ever be blindly loyal. It's important to know when to stand up and say something isn't right and when not to. Pick your battles, because you can't win them all. Always try to be objective and fair-minded when making a decision to be loyal to someone or something. Most of all, make sure your loyalty is in keeping with being true to yourself and your beliefs.

## TRUST

Trusting other people is, by nature, one of the hardest things for any of us to do. I, like many people, have ended up in unenviable situations because we wrongly judged a person as being trustworthy. You've probably confided in someone because it felt safe, only to have them turn around and stab you in the back. I bear many scars from such attacks over the years.

Past experience has taught me to play my cards very close to the vest and you'd do well to do the same. Nowadays, there are only a handful of people who know the real Randy. Erin, you're among those chosen few. I'm fine with the exclusivity I've granted these intimates. They know who they are and have earned my undying trust and respect. As far as I'm concerned, outside of my close circle of confidants, people in general are on a 'need to know' basis. And believe me, there's plenty they don't need to know.

A great example of how I keep things confidential was when your mom and I got married. At the time we both worked for the same company, in the same department. Our marrying was grounds for termination, so it was crucial we kept things quiet. We didn't yet know how we'd handle this aspect of our new life together. We only knew I'd be the one to leave if it came down to it.

Your mom and I had a beautiful wedding at a great restaurant, **The Inn at Lake Waramaug**. I'll never forget it. The setting was very romantic, a small circle of family and friends in attendance. We invited twenty-seven people in total, including one mutual friend who worked with us and could be trusted to keep his mouth shut. Sam ended up acting as my best man. He stood up for us and toasted our success, while some beautiful piano music gently filtered in from an adjoining dining room.

At some point after we were married, word started leaking out at work about our union. The fact these people hadn't found out until after the fateful day kind of softened the blow for everyone involved. After all, it was old news already. There was nothing worthwhile in this discovery to feed the rumor mill, therefore very little interest was shown concerning our new status.

The end result was everyone ended up leaving your mom and me alone to do our jobs. This was what we'd hoped would happen. It was even more satisfying when we discovered a technicality in the company policy. Even though we both worked in the same department, we actually had different supervisors so neither of us could be terminated on the grounds of our marriage alone. That isn't to say they wouldn't have tried had we not handled things exactly as we did. Whew!! What a relief!

Erin, I want you to realize how comfortable it is to be in a position in your life where you have nothing to hide. Where you neither owe anyone anything, nor do they owe you anything in return. It makes it far easier to be a straight shooter and not have to lie about anything. I feel fortunate to be in that kind of position, with that sort of reputation. My hope for you is that you end up in a similar position of respect.

I'm privileged that people confide in me. They know, beyond a shadow of a doubt, what I'm told will stay between us. They also know I'll give them my unbridled opinion, if they ask for it. I treasure this position and hope you someday find yourself in a similar one.

One of the ways I maintain my personal integrity is by considering the possible ramifications of any action or decision I make before I make it - thinking before I leap. You may want to add this to your repertoire.

If you're having difficulty deciding whether something is legal, moral or ethical, consider whether you would want it to be in tomorrow morning's newspaper, on the front page, for the world to see. Would it make you feel proud? Do you truly want others viewing you in that particular light?

> *. . . Life at times can be challenging,*
> *disappointing and even emotionally painful. By*
> *pursuing a loyal, honest and trustworthy path,*
> *the unpleasant experiences you'll face will be*
> *kept to a minimum. You can then focus your*
> *energies on living a more peaceful, productive*
> *and prosperous life, leaving a positive karmic*
> *trail in your wake.*
> *Love,*
> *Dad*

## CHAPTER 5  ESTABLISHING GOALS

"Write it down.  Written goals have a way of transforming wishes into wants; cant's into cans; dreams into plans; and plans into reality.  Don't just think it — ink it!"       Author Unknown

*Dear Erin,*
*In order to be successful and fulfilled in your life,*
*you need to be able to establish personal goals for*
*yourself and work towards attaining them.  Goal*
*setting is a way of defining what your dreams*
*and aspirations are and then creating an outline,*
*spelling out what steps are necessary to achieve*
*them. . . .*

Formulating your personal goals will require intro-spection, deliberation and honesty (don't be afraid to think about what **YOU** really want), as well as some imagina-tion. What things are most important to you? What do you want to achieve in life? Where do you ultimately want to end up? It sounds selfish, doesn't it? Well, it is. But it's important to understand what you want most in life **be-fore** you bring anybody else into the picture.

Let me paraphrase something from an unknown source: Imagine you're in a room with two TV sets: one, a large screen TV with surround sound; the other, a minia-ture screen TV. On which would you tend to focus? Some people make their problems the size of the large screen TV and their personal goals the size of the miniature one. It's important to do the exact opposite: mentally minimize problems and negatives, while maximizing goals and the positives.

Begin by using your imagination to come up with some conceptual ideas. In fact, creative visualization is very important. Imagine yourself in different settings. Let your mind wander and paint different pictures. Then drop yourself into the scene and see how it looks and feels to you.

Then, break your visions down into small components – "who", "what", "when", "where", "how" and "why" are good places to start. With some investigation, elaboration and fine-tuning, your list of goals will be nicely outlined. Once you have things outlined, you can then sort your goals into different categories: short-, medium- and long-term.

When working on your list, be careful not to paint a few broad strokes on the page and call them goals. For example, 'I want to be rich' is not a goal. It's an outcome obtained through achieving goals you set for yourself.

The real work begins with the follow through phase of pursuing your goals. The more you pay attention, keeping your eye on the prize, the more likely you'll be successful. Many people begin by keeping a written list of their goals and reviewing it often so they never lose sight of them.

The commitment needed to achieve your ambitions can seem daunting at times. You'll discover it takes a certain amount of tenacity to see your goals through to the finish line.

Right now, I'm finding I need to fully commit to the task of writing this book, something I've wanted to do for years. It began simply by me making a statement; I felt I should write about my thoughts on life. The actual effort entailed requires far more dedication than I could ever have imagined.

Deciding on and working toward your personal goals is like trying to quit smoking. The human brain is basically lazy and will almost always look for the easy way out. I know when I find time to write, my mind begins to wander. I start thinking of all the things I could be doing that don't require anywhere near as much effort.

If you want to attain your goals, there will be times you'll need to force yourself to work on them. For instance, maybe you'll have a big test coming up and you need to prepare for it, so you forego a party or your favorite TV show. It all depends on what your aspirations are and how serious you are about them; only you can decide what's important for you.

Try not to let the day-to-day noise of life get in the way of working towards your goals, either. Throughout the course of an average day, we're constantly bombarded by things that appear to need immediate attention. It's easy to become overwhelmed and start moving from 'crisis' to 'crisis'. The reality is, most of these issues are nothing more then insignificant nonsense. Try and filter out the truly important things and disregard the rest.

There are certain aspects of your life that should never be ignored or neglected in the pursuit of what you feel you 'need' to be working on. Make it a point never to forsake the people you love, and/or your family, in your quest to achieve an objective. I can't think of anything that should require sacrificing those near and dear to your heart.

I consider myself very goal-oriented. There's a whole array of short-, medium- and long-term objectives on which I'm almost always working. Some may feel it a bit obsessive, but I even have goals surrounding my pastimes like gardening.

Erin, as you know, one of my personal desires is to be able to do some vegetable gardening. This goal has been thwarted by some obstacles these last few years. We sold our old house and ended up waiting far longer than we should have for our new one to be built. Consequently, I've not done any gardening for quite some time. Vegetable gardening was always something I enjoyed, so I decided I needed to start again.

Consumed with my writing and realizing it would be a constant for the foreseeable future, my short term gardening goal for this year was modest. I set up a cold frame so I could grow some leaf lettuce. This will hopefully give us access to fresh lettuce for a greater portion of the year, instead of being limited by the normal growing season. As my fellow gardeners out there know, it's difficult to eat produce that isn't garden fresh once you've grown your own.

My next gardening goal is to fence in an area for a small vegetable plot. I've selected the location - right outside our back door, where we get adequate sun to grow tomatoes. It's an ideal spot for a garden.

Depending on your personal perspective, putting in a vegetable garden next year may not fit the category of a short-term goal. You may think of it as a medium- or even a long-term goal. Our outlooks, priorities and goals may vary. There's no right or wrong. Your self-satisfaction from achieving your goals according to your schedule is what matters.

A long-term gardening goal for me is to set up some hydroponics in the basement. This will happen once I have my cold frame up and running successfully, my vegetable garden in full production and I find I need something new to occupy my time.

Hydroponic gardening will allow me to further increase the variety and availability of our fresh produce. I've given enough thought to this venture that I have an idea of what I'd grow and how I'd go about it, but, because it's a long-term goal, there are still many details to work out. It isn't necessary to finalize my hydroponic gardening plans right now.

Still further down my list of gardening objectives, is to build a small greenhouse. This is more of a dream than any of my other gardening goals; I've only briefly thought about what would be involved. But, my point is, that's okay! You can have goals so far off into the future, focusing on them in the present would be pointless.

My personal gardening objectives are a basic example of goal setting. Short-term objectives should always be the most concrete. They need to be well thought out, analyzed and detailed for the best results. Writing them down is a great way to further add clarity. Long-term goals tend to be more conceptual, or even ethereal, in nature.

There should always be a certain amount of careful, objective thought given to determining if something is a viable goal, or not. The most important consideration should be how achieving said goal will benefit you. Other questions to ask: How much does it cost? What if anything needs to be sacrificed in order to give it more priority? Within what timeframe must it be achieved? Is it something I've always wanted? Will it give me piece of mind and/or self-satisfaction?

There's a group of people who become totally consumed in the game of 'keeping up with the Joneses'- a totally worthless endeavor. They believe if they're successful in owning/doing as much or more than everyone else, they'll be self-satisfied. I never understood this way of thinking. It leaves you with a pile of bills, a house cluttered with things gathering dust and the never-ending quest for more. What's the point? Stay on your personal path to success and don't worry about what others are doing.

In spite of all the best-laid plans, things can change in a New York minute. Life can be moving along as though you were driving down a deserted highway on a gorgeous sunny day, top down, cruising at 85 mph, grooving to the radio, the wind blowing through your hair and, all of a sudden out of nowhere, a deer jumps out in front of your car! What you do next is crucial. Do you panic and act out of fear (which could prove to be fatal), or react calmly and systematically to the situation at hand? Remaining flexible and understanding that there are many aspects of life outside your control will better prepare you for anything that comes your way.

We all have defining moments in our lives. I refer to these events as tectonic in nature based on their suddenness and severity. They almost always necessitate a change in course. As part of your preparation, you'll need two separate sets of personal goals. One set will be goals you can modify and work on regardless of your situation. The second set I refer to as personal dreams; things that would be great to achieve, but are not necessary for self-satisfaction.

One of my long-term personal goals is planning for my retirement. It's something I've been concerned with for several years and I devote a fair amount of time every day to maximizing my return on investments. Fortunately, I enjoy reading business-related material because it can be quite time consuming. For my efforts, I'm beginning to see my nest egg grow. It's time well spent, with gratifying results.

An example of a personal dream of mine would be to do some traveling with your mom when we retire. We both have lists of places we'd love to visit. If things change, we also have a plan B and a plan C. We're ready for wherever the road of life takes us.

> . . . *Erin, your personal agenda, or list of goals, will keep your life from becoming mundane. It's the best way I know of gaining and maintaining a sense of purpose and meaning. As you reach each milestone, your feeling of self-worth, a priceless commodity, will grow. Start creating your road map today.*
> *Love,*
> *Dad*

# CHAPTER 6    SELF-RELIANCE &
# INDEPENDENCE=SELF IDENTITY

"God has given you one face, and you make yourself another."    William Shakespeare


*Dear Erin,*
*Now that you're a teenager, I'm beginning to see*
*the emergence of a young adult with your own*
*unique individual identity; I like what I see.  Your*
*self-reliance and independence are beginning to*
*shine brightly.  Let's talk about how important*
*these traits are and what their development*
*means for you. . . .*

Aside from Ralph Waldo Emerson's essay, 'Self-Reliance', I couldn't find anything worthwhile written about self-reliance or independence. I feel these two intertwined attributes are essential in order for you to become a more substantive adult. They help you to live life on your own terms, attain your full potential and develop a true sense of self.

As you start off on your own path through life, your self-reliance and independence will allow you to take those first scary steps into the unknown. There'll be many new challenges and any achievement, no matter how trivial, will be most gratifying. Accomplishing even menial tasks, such as doing your own grocery shopping or laundry, will feel great. I remember when I learned how to iron my own shirts. I was thrilled that I'd done it by myself for myself.

For most of us during childhood, all of our needs are met. We're provided food, shelter and clothing by our parents and/or other responsible adults. Comfort, reassurance and support are available whenever we're in need. This all makes for a safe, secure and predictable existence doesn't it?

Some young people become complacent with this arrangement, living their lives inside this 'cocoon', accepting little or no responsibility. Think about it: with everything of any consequence provided for, there's little left to do but plan, enjoy and reflect on fun activities.

Eventually, you reach a point where this formula fails to work. You may, even now, begin viewing 'safe and secure' as 'hemmed in and controlled'. Perhaps you sometimes feel smothered, as opposed to nurtured. Frustrating, isn't it? It's all part of growing up, wanting to spread your wings and become independent. Hopefully that won't happen too soon; we like having you around! But your mom and I do realize one day you'll eventually break away from the security we provide and set out on your own. This happens sooner for some than others. It really depends upon the amount of a young person's innate jutzpah. I'm proud to say, you have plenty!

It falls on the shoulders of your mom and me to make sure you're ready to leave the nest, to give you solid roots and wings that'll allow you to soar. Now that you're a teenager, we enjoy watching you begin to assert and define yourself and your place in this world. I view it as practice and preparation for when you face the world on your own. It makes me feel better about your chances for success in your life. I only ask that you don't go about asserting yourself in a rude or disrespectful manner.

When we see you're ready to set out on your own, we'll do everything in our power to help you get underway - the right way. We're firm believers in a grown person's right to be independent. We understand the importance of it.

You, alone, will have to take the initiative when the time is right for fledging the nest. This is exactly where self-reliance and independence are key. Don't let the specter of approval from another person or entity keep you from moving forward with your life.

The sense of free-spiritedness you'll ultimately experience is directly proportional to how willing you are to step outside your comfort zone. Some people are gregarious and adventurous, some are cautious and calculating, and there are countless blends of personality in-between the two.

You mustn't let fear of the unknown get in your way. Fear is always waiting in the wings, ready to take control of your thoughts and actions if you allow it. Instead, you want to look at each and every new experience you face as a new opportunity. Take a deep breath, put one foot in front of the other and see what lies ahead. Don't be afraid to stick your head out and look around corners!

Erin, try to remember that dwelling on any doubts or fears will only make them loom increasingly larger, until they seem insurmountable. The reality is, seldom will any of them be of great magnitude. More often than not, you need only take a step back from a situation and calmly look at it to come up with a viable solution.

Time and experience will help to mitigate much of the anxiety and/or fear you may have when you first start out. For example, if you fear losing your job, prior experience living through such a situation will help ease your trepidation. If you're afraid of losing money, the fact that you've made it before means you'll be able to do it again. There's truly no better education than that obtained from the school of hard knocks. Go out and experience all you can. It can be really exciting!

A self-reliant, independent soul understands and accepts that there will be missteps all along the way. The person who doesn't make mistakes is unlikely to make much of anything at all. As an adventurous person, you'll realize there'll be times when you're in uncharted waters. There won't always be a rulebook you can reference to tell you how something should be handled. Trust in yourself and your gut; use your best judgment and forge ahead.

You may know someone who has no desire to get on with his or her independent life. In fact, some will fight it to the bitter end, kicking and screaming, because they enjoy the comfortable, safe and familiar lives they've been living.

Let me tell you about my friend, Eric, who, after a messy divorce, found himself living back at home with his mom. At first, it was uncomfortable for both of them. Eric's mom was very religious and everything he was in the midst of went completely against her beliefs. She viewed him as a sinner, through and through, but she was also his mother; in spite of her displeasure, she easily slipped into the mothering role once again.

Their mother-son relationship eventually reached a boiling point one evening, when he came home late after being out with friends. He'd been drinking, and tiptoed quietly inside, only to find his mother waiting for him. She literally exploded and uncharacteristically said to him, 'Damn it! You've been relying on me to take care of you long enough. It's time you get out and take care of yourself. Be a man.' Of course, she was absolutely right; he'd been taking advantage of her hospitality and pampering for far too long.

From Eric's perspective, I can understand the appeal of living at home. Having his mom once again provide food and shelter became so comfortable; he'd subconsciously given up the whole idea of ever providing for himself again.

Eric's mom should have kicked him in his butt many years before. Instead, she'd been so content taking care of her son that he'd never been properly 'weaned' from her. I'll venture to guess he ended up getting divorced because his ex-wife didn't want to become his surrogate mommy. You can't get very far in life without taking the reins yourself.

When children aren't raised to have a sense of self-worth and free-spiritedness, they can develop a sense of entitlement. Nothing's more distasteful than having to deal with an adult who thinks the world owes them and they need give nothing back in return. That's why your mom and I are trying to let you spread your wings, gradually. We don't want you taking things for granted, never learning to appreciate the value of work and the satisfaction of earning your own way.

'The Lord helps those who help themselves.' You may be familiar with this old saying. Well, it's really true. Over the years, I've learned how unreliable other people can be when you need them most. With this in mind, I suggest that if you need anything of consequence done, don't entrust it to anyone but yourself. The biggest strides I've ever made in my life were when I took the bull by the horns and just did whatever was necessary to get the job done.

Your independence and self-reliance will allow you to take an active role in where, when and how your life develops. The choices you make will have a profound effect on where life's journey takes you. Imagine all the potential opportunities you'll have presented to you and the decisions you'll make regarding them. The twists and turns in your path through life and how you decide to deal with them will be part of what makes you special and unique.

You don't want to be a spectator of life and live in mediocrity. You want to seize life, be an active participant and live it to the fullest. What's the worst that can happen? You fail! Big deal! We all fail. It's through failure that we learn and become better. No one hits it out of the park every time. As your Aunt Paula likes to say, 'Sometimes you need a base hit'.

Would you really prefer to follow the herd? Being a follower would do nothing more than stunt your personal development, robbing you of uniqueness. Followers don't think for themselves; rather they take the path of least resistance, often doing something because everyone else is doing it. How boring is that? Set out and forge your own path.

One of my favorite movies is 'Under the Tuscan Sun'. Although it was a box office success, it doesn't seem to be very well known. I'd recommend everyone see it as it exemplifies many of the points we're discussing concerning fear and finding your own way.

'Under the Tuscan Sun' is the story of Frances Mayes' journey into a completely new life after suffering through a painful divorce from which her friends think she may never recover. I've watched this movie many times, its impact on me never diminishing. The important lesson taught is to move forward. Just do it!!

Once you're in a position to take care of yourself and your own needs, the self-reliance and independence you've been developing can be channeled and used for achieving ever greater accomplishments. You can start to measure that of which you're truly capable.

Let me tell you about the time I learned how to rappel. Anyone who knows me knows I'm afraid of height. If I'm more than a few feet off the ground, I become uncomfortable. The higher up I go, the more uncomfortable I become. I decided to go rappelling anyway; rationalizing if my friends were willing to try it, I would too.

We went to the Rawley's Bluff near Crystal Lake in Maine. This location offers an entire line of cliffs that mountain climbers from all over the world use to hone their climbing skills. The guy engineering our rappelling experience was a marine on leave who also happened to be an avid mountain climber, with experience as a rappelling instructor as well. While at the base of the cliff discussing the techniques and processes involved, I felt pretty positive about the whole situation.

One important role in rappelling is that of brakeman. A brakeman is stationed at the bottom of the cliff, holding the end of the rope. If the person coming down loses control for any reason, the brakeman simply pulls on the rope stopping them in mid-air; they'll instantly stop descending. Once the climber's situation is assessed, they can slowly be lowered to safety. I was the first brakemen that day.

The first few climbers came down without incident and I served my tour of duty as brakeman basically watching. One person after the next came down the face of the cliff. I started to realize my moment of truth was fast approaching. I was relieved of my brakeman duties and took my turn climbing up the path at the side of the cliff.

The cliff we'd selected was more than 150 feet high with a shear face and a well-worn path up one side. It had seen much use over the years for this type of climbing exercise.

The hike up to the drop point was strenuous, but doable. As I climbed higher, the ground at the foot of the cliff kept growing smaller and smaller. I began to feel a bit anxious, but the anxiety was minimal – so far.

At the top of the cliff, our rappelling instructor greeted me. He quickly and efficiently hooked me up while giving me some last minute instructions. My heart was really POUNDING! I was at the edge and had all I could do to stay focused and not give in to my terror.

In an effort to rationalize my situation and calm myself down, I started thinking about all the safety measures we'd taken. We had received thorough instruction on all the nuances of rappelling. The most calming thought was remembering how many others had already rappelled and made it in one piece. If they could do it, why couldn't I? As I went over the edge, my fear transformed into exhilaration. Wow! I was really going to do it!

The first time down the face of the cliff was a little rough. I kind of just walked down tentatively and slowly. Once I had that first attempt under my belt, I had to do it again... and again... and again. I wanted to really master it. After a few tries, I was bouncing down the side of the cliff like a pro. Our instructor even singled me out and commented on how quickly I'd learned.

For some people, my rappelling experience may seem insignificant. For me, it was huge! I really had to step outside and beyond my limits so I could mentally and physically accomplish it. My independence and self-reliance served me well that day. I had faith in myself and believed I could do it in spite of my fears. That's what it's all about, Erin-pushing your envelope.

The great pitcher, Satchell Paige, used to say, 'Don't look back. Something might be gaining on you.' It's true. Never waste time looking back unless it's to review a lesson previously learned; focus on what's ahead. Let your free-spiritedness drive you. Commit to living a full and fulfilling life. Your Aunt just sent me a great definition for 'commitment': 'When you find a way over every hurdle in your path and nothing but success is an option.'

> . . . *Each of us comes into this world as a unique diamond in the rough. Self-reliance and independence are the tools needed to sculpt you into an original and beautiful work of art. They create the color, shadow and depth of your composition. They are the necessary elements needed to complete your portrait.*
> *Love,*
> *Dad*

## Chapter 7 Affairs of the Heart

"Today I begin to understand what love must be, if it exists. When we are parted, we feel the lack of the other half of ourselves. We are incomplete like a book in two volumes of which the first has been lost. That is what I imagine love to be: incompleteness in absence." Edmond de Goncourt

*Dear Erin,*

*The influence another person can wield over you once they own your heart is immeasurable; the intimate relationships you'll become involved in will have significant impact on your life. I refer to them as affairs of the heart.*

*When it comes to affairs of the heart, it's incredibly important to get it right. A base hit, in this instance, simply isn't enough; you really do want a home run. I hope I can help you identify some key things to look for when choosing a partner; perhaps you can avoid making some of the mistakes I made. . . .*

When you first get involved in a new relationship, everything seems perfect: conversation is plentiful and interesting; time spent together is easy and wonderful. You just can't get enough. Overall, the 'honeymoon phase' of any relationship is effortless and a whole lot of fun.

And let's face it, there's almost always some amount of physical attraction between two people that starts the ball rolling in the first place. At some point sex will come into play, adding another level of discovery and excitement. Be aware, though, sex can also complicate matters. Erin, I hope when you're beginning any new relationship, you keep sex out of the mix until you know your prospective partner as a complete person, without the shroud of sex distorting your view.

For a relationship to begin, the timing has to be just right. Both people need to be mentally and emotionally ready for the commitment involved. You'll only be successful embracing the necessary changes if you're both on the same page.

Erin, I need to caution you against something I've been guilty of more than once in my life. Don't ever jump into a relationship out of desperation or the fear of being alone. At the very least, you'll settle for far less than you deserve; chances are you'll end up in a terrible relationship.

Maintaining the spark and fun in an intimate relationship can be very challenging in the best of circumstances, nearly impossible if things between the two of you aren't right in the first place.

Let's assume everything's going along well. There are some things you can do to help keep it all on track.

Your Aunt and I had a heart to heart conversation several years ago after one of my break-ups. I've never forgotten it. She told me the secret for having a successful relationship really boiled down to two simple rules: **overlook a lot of things** and **treat your significant other like a guest in your home each and every day.**

The more I thought about those two rules, the more I realized Paula was right. For me, abiding by them has made all the difference. Many times they've popped into my head and kept me from saying or doing something regrettable.

Along with these two essential rules, I can't stress enough the importance of truly caring for your significant other's wellbeing. Think about it. If what they do affects you and your life together, how can you not care? If it isn't possible to find it in your heart to care, you most certainly can't share a life together.

Respecting your better half is another essential ingredient for having a successful partnership. Truly liking the person they are is a good place to start. Viewing their thoughts, opinions and feelings as valid is equally as important.

You may be reading this now and rolling your eyes, muttering to yourself, "Of course I should do that!" Knowing it and actually doing it are two totally different things. Doing it requires continual thought and effort. Working on improving your relationship 24/7 is essential when you're in love with somebody. If either or both of you isn't up to the task, cut your losses and walk away.

Many times you're aware there are big problems from the beginning, but you keep hoping things will get better.

It's a well-known fact that many men marry women hoping they'll never change and many women marry men hoping they will. Remember two things: Hope in this case is just a four-letter word and a leopard never changes spots. A healthy relationship is composed of two people who love and accept each other as they are now; two people **willing to work** at creating a meaningful life together.

There are many other things to consider before fully investing in an intimate relationship:

Do you have common interests and backgrounds? Commonality makes it easier to come to a consensus and work together towards a mutually satisfying goal. The ability to discuss different issues and hear your significant other as opposed to arguing with them can make all the difference.

Are you compatible? If the two of you have similar character, values, morals, beliefs and intelligence, relating to one another is much easier. Compatibility will work in conjunction with your commonality, giving you a solid base from which to work in building your lives together.

Can you accept and/or respect each other's political and religious views? Does one or both of you have the need to always be right? Are your incomes disparate? (Unfortunately, this can sometimes be problematic when the woman makes more money than the man.) These are all very important considerations when selecting a partner.

Selfishness knows no place in an affair of the heart. You each must be willing to give 110 percent all of the time. It can no longer be about you-you-you; it will have to be about us-us-us. Your partner's needs should come before yours or at least be on equal footing with yours.

Another prerequisite for any great relationship is genuinely enjoying each other's company. It's not enough to simply like someone. I like many people but can only tolerate them in small doses. Life's too short to spend time with people whose company you don't enjoy. Ask yourself this: Would you be able to sit through a dinner with them? Would you even invite them to dinner in the first place?

If you're in a solid relationship, when the two of you are apart you should still be able to function as independent human beings. I'm sure you've seen some 'happy' couples that need to always call their partner before doing anything. I think that's ridiculous. You need to be able to trust your mate to make some decisions and assumptions on their own, without you being their puppet master.

Effective communication within a relationship is vital. It's a way of providing care and comfort, as well as helping you become more familiar with each other. I'd recommend, at some point each day, the two of you have some uninterrupted conversation. I mean turn off the TV or music, sit together and give each other your undivided attention. Your mate will appreciate a sympathetic and compassionate ear. Don't sit there and do all the talking. Listen to every little detail of whatever they want to talk about, for however long is needed.

The bible says 'Everyone should be quick to listen, slow to speak, and slow to get angry'. No truer words were ever spoken. Let me add you should also be polite. Remember to say please and thank you. It's a pleasant, subtle way of letting your significant other know you 'heart' them.

Make it a point to be complimentary: 'I really like your hair today'; 'I love those shoes'; 'Dinner was really good honey'; 'I love that outfit on you; 'That recipe's a keeper! Really good!' I think you get the idea.

A tricky part of communicating with your mate is telling them when something isn't great. It can be extremely difficult to get your point across without hurting their feelings. At times, it'll seem like you're trying to tip-toe through a minefield. First, determine whether it's important to make them aware of your dislike. If it's just an oddball, one-in-a-million situation, it may be better to bite your tongue. Think before you speak.

Never be afraid to say 'I love you'. The power within those three little words is incredible. Tell your significant other you love them often enough that they know beyond a shadow of a doubt. Don't ever think you're telling them too often. Just be sure it's heartfelt and that they hear you.

Some people have difficulty saying 'I love you.' Maybe they were brought up in an environment where the words were used rarely or not at all. They may feel saying 'I love you' will make them appear weak. Maybe saying 'I love you' will make them feel vulnerable. This means you'll have to draw them out of their shell over time. Don't give up! Those three words can soften the hardest and coldest of hearts.

True love doesn't mean you need to be ignorant of your significant other's wrongs. It also doesn't mean you wave them in their face as a constant reminder. If you feel like your partner has done something wrong that you may not agree with, discuss it without yelling, screaming, or name-calling. (Just think about how you've felt in the past when someone has called you a name. It can be devastating.)

No one can tell you who the right significant other for you is. It's something you have to feel inside. The gender of the person in relation to yours is of minor consequence. While I'm not one to promote homosexuality, I do believe in the saying, 'To each his own'. I certainly don't believe the government should get in the way of this choice either. While I define marriage as the union of a man and a woman, that doesn't mean gay couples should be iced out because of it. They're entitled to their own happiness; I wish everyone would just let them be. Remember the old adage 'Behind every good man is a good woman'. It should be rewritten to read, 'Behind every great person is an even greater significant other'.

Another thing I'd like to bring up concerning intimate relationships is they should always be progressing, moving towards some next step. Hopefully the next step is a positive one, adequately communicated and agreed upon by both parties involved. Often this means reaching a mutually satisfying compromise (easier said than done). If this isn't achieved, sooner or later the relationship will be negatively impacted. One of the parties often ends up feeling cheated or disrespected by, or subordinate to, the other.

You can't reverse a relationship's direction either. Let's say two people break up because things between them didn't seem to be working. After a time apart, the emotional wounds start to heal and they decide to give it another try. Remembering a leopard never changes spots and the two essential rules I wrote about earlier in this chapter, reconciling couples need to think long and hard concerning exactly what their relationship will need to better mesh the second time around. It'll require much concession between the parties if they ever expect it to work out. My advice to people in this position is not to look back and try to reconcile. Even though it seems like a safe and familiar place, more often than not it won't be a happier one.

When you're in an intimate relationship for a long period of time, your level of security within it will increase. This often allows its progression to occur more subtly. Your relationship goals start to become longer term in nature, with more gradual transitions.

Maybe you and your significant other will start to talk about what you want to spend your time doing once the kids move out. Or maybe even what your golden years should be like together. There's no set pace for how a relationship will develop. It simply must be proceeding along so both parties are happy and satisfied.

There's an adage, 'Love means never having to say you're sorry'. While it may be nice to believe love can conquer all, I think this idea is flawed. If you respect and care about your significant other's feelings, you'll be able to say you're sorry. Remember, you should be working towards the greater good, the health and wellbeing of your life together.

The ability to say you're sorry is only part of the equation, not holding a grudge is another. You can't have a long memory concerning things said or done by your partner that may have been hurtful to you. If you love and care for them and they love you in return, learn to let things go. Chalk it up as a forgettable miscue. Everyone has a bad day!

Sometimes the most insignificant things between you and your better half can have monumental implications. For example, a comment expressed in conversation could turn around and have a major impact on how you view each other from that point on. It could prove to help cement your relationship or drive a wedge in it. Hopefully you have enough of a foundation together where there will be no lasting damage caused by stupidity or ignorance. Try and be aware of what I like to call your partner's hot buttons.

Every person has at least one hot button, some little thing that can drive them insane by mere mention. For example, your mom knows she's a procrastinator. At times she's even bothered by that fact. It's simply not in her nature to be bothered by things she considers inconsequential. I accept this facet of her personality and can usually deal with it, unless it affects the resolution of an issue I consider important.

I could make your mom's procrastination a much larger issue than it is, but I don't because I love her and it's part of the package I signed up for when I married her. If you discover what your partner's hot buttons are, don't push them. Simply learn to accept and live with their foibles.

In order to have a healthy and successful relationship, there must be a balance between all these things I've written about, along with mutual agreement of what that balance should be. For example, sex may be of paramount importance for some couples and not for others. Establish together what aspects are most important in your relationship.

I want to issue a note of caution here regarding sex. Some people feel it should be the most important part of a relationship. Well Erin, I hope there's more to your relationship than that. If not, I'm afraid you could be in for a rude awakening. Guess what? There will come a day when the sex won't play as big a role; one or both of you will run out of gas. Then what?

> *. . . Erin, I hope reading what I've written here will help you have a more fulfilling love life. If I can lessen the bumps and bruises and pave the way for you to find true happiness, I'll be a happy father.*
> *Love,*
> *Dad*

# CHAPTER 8    THOUGHTS ON PARENTING

If your children look up to you, you've made a success of life's biggest job."          Author Unknown

*Dear Erin,*
*Parenting's a difficult topic for me to write about.  I feel like I've had success and failure in my role as a father, which might leave you wondering why I'd offer any advice at all. . . .*

Well, I'm quite certain many parents end up feeling this way. The nature of parenting is such that it's often difficult to tell how well you're doing. In fact, it could be years before you get a true indication. The thrill of victory and the agony of defeat are ever present.

Having said all that, I hope my impressions and opinions, both good and bad, might provide you with some insight as to what you might expect when the time comes that you're a parent.

By far, the biggest failure of my life has been my father-son relationship with your brother. I've not seen or heard from him for several years. He's the casualty of my failed marriage to his mother.

Conversely, I was an active stepfather to your sister. I'm proud to say I played some part in her development.

Then, of course, there's you. At fifteen you're growing up to be a very attractive, intelligent and personable young woman. You don't seem to follow the crowd to the same degree other kids your age do. I like that. Seeing you develop a sense of self is very satisfying for me. Though the jury's still out, I'd like to think that your mom and I have been successful where you're concerned.

The end result for many parents will be just as mixed. Some kids turn out okay; some don't. Some parental guidance will be heeded; some won't. As a parent, all you can ever really do is your very best and pray a lot.

There are many facets to being a good parent. Before we talk about them, it's important to understand parental perspective: Our good judgment comes from experience. Our experience comes from bad judgment.

Parents don't want their kids suffering by making the

same mistakes they did. My goal is to guide you and prevent you from making serious missteps. It sounds simple enough, doesn't it?

Being a good parent requires an incredible amount of patience - far beyond anything I thought I could ever muster. That isn't to say you're a bad kid or any kid's a bad kid. It's simply a case of you wanting what you want, when you want it, right or wrong, even if your mom and I are diametrically opposed to it. It can be extremely frustrating to deal with children who don't fully comprehend right from wrong and who aren't yet capable of understanding the ramifications of and answering for the things they say and do.

Throughout the parenting process, it's very difficult to maintain a balance between good guy and bad guy. There's often a very fine line between being patient, loving and tolerant, and being a strict disciplinarian. And remember, more often than not your kids will find fault with whatever course of action you've taken.

The highs and lows of parenting are a lot like a roller coaster ride with all the high-speed ups and downs, as well as some unexpected curves thrown in for good measure. Throughout it all, it's your job as a parent to continue maintaining the unconditional love you have for your kids.

You'll often hear unconditional love comes naturally in a parent-child relationship. I disagree. Love can require a lot of effort when children throw temper tantrums, bombard you with verbal abuse, have repeat run-ins with the law, etc. Be prepared; sooner or later, **every** child takes his or her turn at bad behavior.

It's unhealthy to dwell on the day-to-day fluctuations in any of your close, personal relationships, especially those with your kids. There will be periods, sometimes lasting several years, where tensions can and do exist. All you can do is offer to be there whenever you're needed. This is especially true as your kids get older and start looking for more independence.

Keeping the lines of communication open between you and your children can be quite challenging as they grow older. They naturally want to do more and more on their own without having to rely on mom and dad. Many kids shut themselves off from their parents, creating and living in their own little world within the family home environment. The more ways you can find to keep them an active part of the family, the less likely this is to happen.

It becomes increasingly difficult to allow your kids more freedom as they grow older. Kids, especially teenagers, tend to overlook that their parents were once young too. There isn't much any kid can dream up that hasn't been done before. There aren't many parents who find calm in that.

Some parents have a hard time accepting the idea that no child, especially a teenager, should be trusted all the time. Being truthful and letting parents in on absolutely everything just isn't part of a teenager's DNA. It's important to remain ever vigilant in monitoring children's activities.

When problems arise, it's helpful for parents to attempt understanding the issue at hand as fully as possible, seeing it from all sides. Much like a judge hearing a case, the goal is to remain impartial and fair-minded. In order to be objective, you'll need to maintain a level of empathy with your children. When situations are emotionally charged, this can be challenging.

It can be very difficult for parents to watch their kids grow up. It happens so fast; one day your little girl is a young woman, beginning to build a life of her own. As a parent, it's important to fade off into the background a bit, so children can get on with their own lives. It's essential they learn how to function on their own and make their own decisions. It's easier to let go a little at a time than to try to let go all at once.

Many parents don't want their kids to grow up and leave the nest because they fear being alone and facing their own mortality. It can be a pretty scary time if you've spent your entire adult life ignoring your own wants and needs, while you raise your children. Don't forsake who you are while caring for others.

Some parents try to control every aspect of their kid's lives. Dissatisfied with their own childhood, thinking in terms of should've, would've and could've, they decide to live vicariously through their kids by orchestrating all their activities. Nothing good ever comes of this.

As you know, your mom and I have consistently urged you to do something with your singing voice and creative writing abilities. In the end it'll be your choice. We'll love and support you in whatever path you decide to take - **no matter what**.

. . .*Erin, there's been a lot written about
parenting to better relate to your kids and create
a more zen-like existence with them. That's all
fine, but don't ever lose sight of what a parent's
role is. You're there to nurture and protect them.
Your goal is to make them all they can be.
Here's hoping you end up being a great mom!
Love,
Dad*

## Chapter 9   Education

"Education is the knowledge of how to use the whole of oneself. Many men use but one or two faculties out of the score with which they are endowed. A man is educated who knows how to make a tool of every faculty—how to open it, how to keep it sharp, and how to apply it to all practical purposes."   Henry Ward Beecher

*Dear Erin,*
*I never thought I'd find myself writing what has been said repeatedly by others, but here I go. . . .*

I can't stress enough the importance of a good education. Aside from caring for your health, getting a good education may be the most important thing you can do for yourself. You'll find you're viewed as insignificant and forgettable in today's world without one. Chances are you won't even be able to get a decent job.

Without a good job you probably won't be able to adequately take care of yourself, much less your family; you won't be able to afford all that life has to offer. And although you're not supposed to marry for money, just try finding anyone who'll be interested in you if you don't earn, or have the potential to earn, a decent living. You'll end up being viewed as more of a liability than a prospect.

First things first: it's essential you graduate from high school. I know how pointless high school can seem (been there, done that), but it's a necessary rite of passage into adulthood. You could be the most talented, likeable person on Earth, but, without a high school diploma, you'll be judged negatively and many doors of opportunity will remain closed to you. The stigma attached to being a high school dropout is like having 'FAILURE' stamped across your forehead.

Having said all that, in today's world it isn't enough to have a high school diploma. You'll need much more on your resume in order to compete for decent employment. You have to maximize your education wherever you can, your goal being to distinguish yourself from the masses. This means you need to do extra things to be noticed and/or to showcase whatever skills and talents you have.

A good example would be your sister. She graduated with a degree in Medical Technology and proceeded to take the additional classes required to obtain a second degree in Biology. How many people can say they have two Bachelor's degrees? Think about how valuable she'll look in an employer's eyes.

Don't forget extra-curricular school activities either. Get involved in things like the drama club, chorus and sports. Put forth whatever extra effort is needed to get your teachers to take notice of you. You never know when a recommendation from one of them will be the deciding factor in you being awarded a scholarship or not.

I decided I wanted to go to college after being out of school for many years. I felt I needed to do something more with my life and my career. At first, almost everyone I knew thought I would just take a couple classes and be done with it, but I'm not the type of person who starts things without finishing them.

As I started accumulating credits, I reached a point where I needed to formally enroll in one of the college programs. I matriculated into the Electrical Engineering program.

Within short order, I found I was a good college student. I was living on my own, supporting myself and working full-time, so studying was challenging. Tuition, fees and books were also extremely difficult to afford, but I did it. I only wish I'd done it all years earlier; things would have been so much easier.

I ultimately graduated with honors maintaining a 3.53 cumulative average. Not too shabby having selected one of the most difficult and math driven two-year curriculums there was at the time. Remember what I said about standing out from others? One of my instructors saw potential in me and recommended me as a candidate to continue my education at M.I.T. What an honor!

Although I chose not to pursue a career based on my college degree, I learned a lot about myself: I was reasonably intelligent; I could be a good student and a quick study if I put my mind to it; and I'm analytical and adaptable by nature. Believe me when I say, anything that teaches you about yourself is a worthwhile venture.

Earning your college degree shows everyone that you have discipline, commitment and brainpower. You'll be judged positively and new doors of opportunity will be open to you. It will be as though you have 'SUCCESS' stamped across your forehead.

Let's talk about how I hope you'll go about your own college experience. Erin, let me start off by saying I hope you pay attention in high school and get good enough grades to be considered college worthy. High school is where you need to show your teachers you have potential. Believe it or not, they're paying attention. That's why you get graded. Things such as doing your homework, not being absent or tardy, good test scores , extra-curricular activities and community volunteer work comprise your transcript (scholastic resume'). You'd be amazed at how much detail can be found about you with one phone call.

Next you want to begin thinking about what kind of college you want to attend and what course of study you wish to pursue. The decisions you make at this juncture are not carved in stone, in spite of what you may hear to the contrary. You can begin your college education and not declare a major until your junior year. Most of the classes you take early on are core courses, required of everyone.

Once you declare a major or matriculate into a college program of study, you can still change your mind; it may just mean it'll take you longer to get your degree. Who cares if you have to go back and take some additional courses? Any and all learning will only benefit you.

Don't let other people throw barriers in your way when it comes to getting a college education. You're the only person who can say what you want to do and what's right for you. You need to really want something in order to be successful. The keys are desire, dedication and determination.

I've seen countless kids go to college only to waste their time and their parents' money. Perhaps the sense of entitlement I've written about came into play. Who knows? I've also experienced the hard-earned reward of paying for my own education. I was fully invested; I understood the value. The pay-off was great.

You have to demonstrate that you want a college education. Your mom and I will help you financially and otherwise, but there's no free ride. You'll need to put forth the effort and make the sacrifices. You'll have to work hard and earn it, to be invested and understand the value. Following this formula, your pay-off will be great.

Having a partial financial stake in your education buys you some flexibility. Your mom and I don't want to pressure you into choosing any specific educational or career path. That decision should be yours alone.

Erin, something else I need to mention regarding education is the importance of not studying subjects that are no longer viable in today's world. I don't mean you shouldn't learn more about the things you love. You're practical enough to realize the purpose of getting a college education is to enable you to get a decent, well-paying job, hopefully in a career you love.

When I signed myself back into high school, I wanted to do something more than simply muddle my way through the typical classes like Social Studies. I wanted to learn something that would help me get a job when I graduated. One of the options open to high school juniors and seniors was a career training program.

This trade school option was where high school age kids would spend 1000 hours in each of their junior and senior years learning trades in the hope of becoming employable upon graduation. The training offered was in such fields as carpentry, plumbing and cosmetology, to name but a few.

One of the courses offered at the time was Offset Printing & Lithography. The trade school had recently invested more then $250,000.00 into this program and was pushing it as one of their premier offerings.

Shortly after getting involved in the program, I began hearing from other trade school students how I'd been sold a bill of goods. I was wasting my time learning 'a dying trade'. I felt like I had to live with my choice because there weren't any openings in anything else that held my interest. It turned out to be a poor decision.

As I was finishing up my second year of printing, a BIG problem became evident. Computers were quickly eliminating the need for printers in general. Entire print shops were being replaced by a handful of people and their computers. I graduated high school having learned a dying trade, virtually unemployable.

Don't let this happen to you! Make sure you do plenty of research as to which careers will be in demand ten or fifteen years from now. For example, health care, alternative fuels and agriculture are projected to be growing areas in which ample employment opportunities will be available for the next decade or more. A college degree in any one of these fields promises a future to those who are interested.

It's important you also select a career path with abundant opportunities, as opposed to opportunities for a select few. For example, I wouldn't recommend something in Art History or Philosophy, even though there may be some demand for people with this background. Yes, there'll be some opportunities; however, they'll be very few and far between.

I would also urge you to stay away from career fields like law, accounting and medicine with over-abundant, well-trained workforces already in place, as well as a whole crop of new graduates ready and waiting in the wings. Vying for jobs in these areas can be very competitive, even downright cutthroat. I don't want you ending up in the shark pool! It'll be many years before there's a genuine need for more individuals in these areas of business.

> . . . *Erin, to sum up, you want to select a career path in an up and coming industry, with plenty of opportunities and a variety of different jobs. The icing on the cake is when you find your niche and end up doing something that's personally gratifying while earning a good salary.*
> *Love,*
> *Dad*

# CHAPTER 10  COPING IN THE WORK PLACE

"The butt you Kick today may be the butt you Kiss tomorrow."  Author Unknown

*Dear Erin,*
*As I write this, our country is in the midst of the most severe economic downturn since the great depression of the 1930's.*
*It began as a seemingly insignificant problem with sub-prime home mortgages.  A combination of politics and greed created an environment of unsustainable spending.*
*People, who by rights should not have been allowed to buy homes, were given the opportunity to do so via lowered credit standards.  Then, the flawed belief home values would never decrease allowed anybody and everybody to use their perceived home equity to fuel further buying on credit. Home equity was being used as a virtual ATM machine.*

Eighteen months later, the entire world found itself in
what's being called a severe protracted recession. Some
even say we're on the brink of a depression that'll last
several years.

Even though our family lives in a relatively conservative
manner, we've been sucked into the economic morass.
It's Monday, March 16, 2009 and I'm home, as I will be
every Monday for the foreseeable future. The company
I'm working for is trying to survive the economic downturn
by cutting costs. We now work a four-day week, meaning
my pay has been cut twenty percent. Initially, I was very
upset by this; however, it's proving to have both advan-
tages and disadvantages.

The obvious disadvantage is dealing with a twenty percent pay cut. In the first few weeks I thought I would just
go out and get a part-time job to make up the difference.
While I still have hopes of finding something more to help
financially, it doesn't look like it'll happen anytime soon.
The building and remodeling industries seem to have
come to a dead stop. About all your mom and I can do for
the time being is tighten our belts.

One advantage of my shortened work schedule is I finally
have the opportunity to do some writing. The timing
couldn't be better, especially as I try to put my thoughts
on coping in today's working world down on paper. It
gives me an opportunity to review things I thought I'd forgotten about during my forty-three years of life in the
workforce. It also may give you food for thought to better
cope with your upcoming journey into the business world.
Let me start out with a review of my work life so you have
a better understanding of where I'm coming from with my
views and opinions. . . .

As you probably already know, I started working when I was twelve years old. I became a paperboy. This is when I got my social security card. I was going to make some legitimate money and learn what it meant to be responsible for something other than myself.

Neither rain, nor snow, heat nor cold kept me from delivering my newspapers. I had sixty some odd customers relying on me and I never let them down. At times, it was really tough to follow through, but I had a responsibility to make my daily deliveries. Believe me, there's nothing like having to go outdoors at the crack of dawn, on a Sunday morning in the middle of the winter, when you have the extra heavy Sunday newspaper to collate and deliver. It would take hours. In spite of what, at times, seemed to be insurmountable difficulties, I did my job and my customers loved me. I got great tips at Christmas time, which was the measure of success back then.

I had a couple other jobs along with the paper route as well. I mowed one of my neighbor's lawns. I even picked up a snow shovel and tried to make money with that once in awhile. I can't say I'd recommend shoveling snow to a kid looking to make money, though; we all know how back breaking it can be.

Erin, you're a young adult, about to enter the working world. There are some basics you need to have in order to be a success right out of the gate. These are things many people should be aware of, yet often seem to ignore.

Basic elements for successfully starting out in the working world include: a neat appearance, punctuality and diligence, as well as the desire and ability to learn how to do the job. You'll also need to be able to get along with others, including those within your company whom no one else can handle.

Once you begin establishing yourself in a new job, you'll be assessed to see if you have 'the right stuff'. Along with the qualities I've already mentioned, your employer will be concerned with how you fit overall into their 'culture'. Are you friendly? Do people like you in return? How are you adjusting? Are you adaptable to changing conditions? How do you deal with stress and deadlines?

During the initial stages of your job, your employer will scrutinize everything about you and what you do. If you leave any doubt in their mind concerning your abilities and/or fit in their organization, you could be released without any reason given (usually within the first 90 days). It's easier to cut someone loose before they end up a part of your company's benefits (i.e. Health insurance, 401K plan, etc.) and/or they start putting down roots.

Let's say you make it through the initial ninety-day 'tire kicking' stage as a new employee. Your employer must have seen some promise in you. Now, you'll be scrutinized on your job performance. Every little thing you do will be dissected. Even if you aren't aware of it, assume you're being watched. Be sure to dot all your i's and cross all your t's. Don't take anything for granted or assume you're safe.

Based on my experience in the business world, it takes at least 18 months for you to really start settling in on a job. With that much time under your belt, you can probably do a competent job and other employees will have adjusted to working with you. It's important these two things happen if you want to be assured of any kind of job security and, more importantly, if you want to be promoted.

Okay Erin, let's say you've begun making your mark at your job; you've successfully created a niche for yourself within the company. Your employer will start throwing more responsibility your way to better fully assess the stuff of which you're made. He or she will look for the invaluable traits that could transform you into one of their 'go to' people.

Beyond fitting into the company culture, being genuinely likeable, adaptable, diligent and willing to learn, there are other invaluable employee traits. Let's look at some of them.

Two of the most important qualities that work in tandem are your abilities to manage your time effectively and complete projects on or before the target dates. Often in the work place, when you're hired for a job there's very little, if any, formal training. It'll be your responsibility to figure out how to go about your job and get everything done. You'll need to discern which things take priority and learn to work systematically and efficiently.

Once you've established your priorities, work on completing them one at a time. A past employer once told me something I've never forgotten: 'Use a rifle not a shotgun'. Finish one project before moving on to the next (unless you can't because you're missing information). Don't be distracted by anything else.

This doesn't mean you won't ever be called upon to multi-task, a common cause of stress in the workplace. Unexpected problems will rear their ugly heads, demanding immediate attention. It'll be important for you to prove you can deal with these 911's while still keeping your primary job under control. Of course, if these 'bumps in the road' happen with any regularity, other plans of action may be necessary.

Remember something about bosses in general. You'll seldom hear from them if you're doing a good job; you'll hear plenty when you make an error, particularly if your mistake costs the company money. So, once you've figured out how to go about your job, don't ever expect to receive any kind of pat on the back.

Discretion and confidentiality are two more traits your employer will be looking for in you. They don't appreciate gossip, busy bodies or drama queens. If they know you can keep things quiet, you'll start to become more of a confidante, as opposed to simply an employee. People enjoy working with someone in whom they can put their faith and trust.

Another sought after trait looked for in employees is honesty. I know how ridiculous this may sound to you, but it's in short supply in the business world. While political correctness is nice, over the years I've found that employers like the fact when I'm asked a direct question, and I know the entire conversation will be kept confidential, they'll get an honest response. If you can't trust your employer to keep things confidential, bite your tongue. Anything you say can and most probably WILL be used against you.

Being a team player, helping out where you can, is another desirable characteristic looked for by employers. This can be a little frustrating at times when you're doing your job and always picking up the slack for others who aren't keeping pace. A team roster is never made up entirely of rock stars.

I'll help out whenever and wherever I'm able, but I usually request that attention not be drawn to it. I like establishing myself within the company as someone who can be counted on to get the job done without fanfare, no matter what! Some might not agree with this, feeling that calling attention to themselves and their achievements is important. Believe me when I tell you, your boss will probably know who's actually doing their job and who's coasting.

You'll quickly discover how many people in the working world aren't the team players they profess to be. These are the individuals who push to make themselves look good, grabbing headlines wherever and whenever possible. They'll use you and/or throw you under the bus for their own personal gain. Identify them and handle them with kid gloves. Stay clear of them entirely, if at all possible.

While we're on the subject of the different types of co-workers you'll encounter on the job, let me mention a couple types of co-workers you'll want to stay away from if at all possible (unless your boss fits one of these categories). I call them 'bomb throwers' and 'dump trucks'.

A bomb thrower is a co-worker who loves to see you sweat, so they go out of their way to produce obstacles for you to overcome. They continually lob live grenades in your direction so **they** don't have to deal with any thorny issues; and at the same time they get to see you suffer.

A 'dump truck' is a co-worker who loves to pass off all of their work on anybody they can. This way they rid themselves of performance stress, as well as any possible blame for not meeting crucial deadlines. Their response to a boss's query will usually be something like: 'I gave it to Dave to take care of last week'. The true 'dump trucks' go about their business so naturally, they often don't know how detrimental they are to the rest of the team.

Beware of tasks that present themselves under the guise of volunteering. Don't get sucked into doing some ungodly thing that no one else will do, unless it's something management really wants done and would be appreciative of you tackling.

One of the annoying things I've encountered repeatedly on the job is my co-workers spending a lot of energy worrying about what the boss is doing: where they're going, what kind of car they drive, the type of house they live in, etc. Forget all that! It's simply nobody's business. I've told my co-workers many times and I'll tell you, 'I don't care who does what, who does who, or who's doing what to who, as long as it doesn't affect my family and/or me. When you work for someone, 'Yours is not to reason why; yours is but to do or die'. If you can't sign on for that, look for employment elsewhere.

Another reason for changing jobs is if the time has come where you can no longer learn anything new and/or expand your role any further. The minute either happens for a protracted length of time, you need to move on and look for new opportunities. Don't stay at your job if you're simply going through the motions.

It's crucially important to maintain a balance between your career and personal life so neither one is harmed by the other. This balance will be different from person to person and couple to couple. One way of weighing it is by determining how much of an income you want (one side of the scale) and how much you're willing to tolerate in order to earn it (the other side of the scale).

There's a principle that comes into play here known as, "The Peter Principle". First postulated by Dr. Laurence Peter and Raymond Hull in the late sixties, it says that a worker will continue being promoted until they reach their individual level of incompetence. It also states the majority of actual work is done by workers who haven't yet reached this plateau.

Don't be so career-driven that you end up pushing relentlessly to attain this level of success. Work instead on attaining a healthy balance between your professional and personal lives.

It took me a long time to figure out this balancing act. I can't tell you how many times a younger Randy literally killed himself trying to achieve totally unrealistic results in an effort to please an authority figure. Sacrificing your personal ideals and beliefs is a fool's game. Just say no!! A paycheck is never worth prostituting yourself, unless what you want for yourself is to be a prostitute. In that case, I say be the best one out there.

This may be a good time for me to mention a couple unique opinions I have about the workplace. They're based on my experience in the business world wearing many different hats, at various levels, in companies of all different sizes. Even though my thoughts may seem slightly unorthodox, I'm confident you'll find merit in them, given time to digest them.

An expression I've told many of my co-workers over the years when they find themselves in unenviable no-win positions is, 'Always remember **S.P.A.M.** - **S**wallow your **P**ride **A**nd **M**ove forward.

Your boss and/or co-workers may occasionally make unreasonable requests of you. Whether they're genuinely unreasonable in nature, or just unacceptable to you, this happens.

Even if you have the most wonderful boss in the world and have worked for the company for several years, sooner or later you'll be asked to do something you absolutely hate. You'll need to catch yourself and think before acting or speaking, so you don't magnify the moment or issue into some career-altering catastrophe. If you value your job, just suck it up and get the unpleasant task over with.

It's of paramount importance to work for someone you respect and a company in which you believe. It makes dealing with your job much easier if you feel good about where you work and what you're doing. If you're the least bit uneasy about how the company's operating, don't belabor the issue; get another job.

After you've worked for a time in the corporate world, you'll begin to understand how decisions are usually made. I like to kid around about this formula, but unfortunately it seems to hold true more often than not.

There seems to be two basic rules that must be applied to any possible decision before it can be implemented at the corporate level. Both conditions must be met, or this possible solution will be thrown out and another considered. These two rules are:

# 1 - It must make absolutely no sense at all.

# 2 - It must cause extreme discomfort to someone within the organization.

These criteria come into play within a corporate environment for many reasons. First there are usually far too many chiefs involved in the decision-making process. With so many people entangled in establishing workplace guidelines, whatever new initiatives are instituted end up watered down and ineffective. The desired outcome as originally conceived is often lost in the process. Many times these new policy mutations end up serving as roadblocks employees need to work around in order to continue getting their jobs done.

To make matters worse, most people in a corporate environment will make decisions that insure their own job security, often putting the company's welfare second or even third. Additionally, these decision makers may have friends or allies within the company whose jobs they're also trying to protect.

This decision making process is not limited to the employees of a company. Often the upper echelon of the management team will function in this same quid pro quo manner. Favoritism is very much in play among the power brokers of any company regardless of size and/or stature.

This attitude is almost impossible to ignore or avoid. Some people are much more influenced by this 'selfish' attitude than others, but it's the norm in a corporate environment. I only wish company CEO's would recognize that, with few exceptions, they can't count on their management teams to be anything more than 'yes men'.

Be very selective in any battles you choose to fight in the workplace. It just isn't possible to win them all. If you constantly complain and/or try to make your grievances known, people will stop listening or even find a way to get you out of their hair and out the door. Remember the boy who cried wolf?

When selecting a battle to fight, avoid any 'holy grail' subjects. These are untouchable policies or circumstances that usually end up in place because of the company's history and tradition, 'We always did it this way'.

It's important you make yourself and your name memorable to all your business contacts. This includes employers, potential employers, co-workers, associates and clients. You should always put your best foot forward and leave some kind of lasting mark. When people think of you, they need to feel good about it. A good reputation can take years and be very expensive to acquire, only to be easily lost if you're careless.

What you choose to do for a living is not nearly as important as striving to be the very best you can be. Look at your Opa. He's someone who truly loves working with wood and he's spent his life following his passion. To this day when someone is looking for him, he'll undoubtedly be found in his shop, making something. That's a litmus test for you. Do you really love what you're doing for a living? Would you do it even if you weren't getting paid?

> *. . . Erin, always remember, a job well done is a source of pride.*
> *Love,*
> *Dad*

## CHAPTER 11   HOW TO CONDUCT AN EFFECTIVE JOB SEARCH

"In life, change is inevitable, yet everyone resists it. Remember this: When you're through changing, you're through."   Author Unknown

*Dear Erin,*

*I want to offer you some ideas on how to conduct an effective job search, should the need ever arise for you. One thing my recent job lay-off reminded me of was never take your job for granted. Even if you're a highly skilled, well-liked worker with a proven track record, that's no guarantee of continued employment. You always need to be prepared in the event the rug, suddenly and unexpectedly, gets pulled out from under you. Monday, June 15, 2009 found me at home trying to figure out what steps I should take in my quest to find employment. . . .*

After working for more than seven years at a prestigious kitchen and bath design firm, I found myself among the ranks of the unemployed. The reason I was given for my lay-off was lack of business at the firm; however, office politics almost always comes into play when the 'powers that be' decide who should be next on the chopping block. Higher paid, less qualified employees remained in my wake. That felt like a slap in the face.

While I was assured being unemployed in the current economic environment was nothing to be ashamed of, it still felt degrading. I began to doubt myself and my talents. Even having a great resume' didn't make me feel better. The only thing I wanted to hear was, "You're hired!"

The country was in the midst of a spectacular economic downturn. The company I'd been working for was attempting to survive the current recession by cutting costs. While the kind of work I did was beneficial in helping the company maximize profit, there's no profit when there's no business. I became an unnecessary expense.

My last day of employment was Friday June 12, 2009. The company owner, accompanied by the acting Operations Manager, arrived at the showroom around 7:00 A.M. They unceremoniously released me, handing me a copy of a separation agreement they wanted signed. I took it home with me.

My first week out of work was spent tying up the loose ends I had with my now former employer, updating my resume' and filing for unemployment. I wasn't ready to put on a happy face and go out looking for work, so it proved to be the perfect time to take care of these things. I'd recommend others do the same. It takes at least a few days to get used to the idea of being out of work without the emotional upset that brings.

In over twenty-five years, I'd never needed my resume' to get a job, so my resume' was in desperate need of up-dating. The challenge was to adequately showcase my experience, skills and accomplishments, while keeping it readable and no longer than two pages. With your mom's help, I was sending out the first copies of my resume' to prospective employers before the end of week one. **Erin - rule number one: Always keep your resume' up to date.** Whether you're employed or not, you never know when you may need it. You're dead in the water without one.

Tying up loose ends with my former employer involved the separation agreement they wanted signed and re-turned by July 15th. I'd never been given one before, but it's fairly commonplace in today's work environment. Em-ployers are concerned you'll sue them when they release you, so they dangle the carrot of severance pay in front of you on the condition you sign one of these.

I promptly called my attorney and drove the agreement down to his office for review. I didn't want any delay; I wanted my severance pay. I also wanted to know where I stood legally.

My attorney and I discussed the separation agreement; he thought its content seemed pretty stan-dard. I expressed my concern about how prospective em-ployers might perceive me being laid off after seven years with the company. I asked him what he thought about notifying my former employer that I'd sign and return the agreement in exchange for letters of recommendation. He thought it was a great idea.

I arranged to drop off the signed agreement and pick up the letters in person. **Erin - rule number two: You want to get letters of recommendation whenever you can and keep them on file for yourself.**

Something else I addressed during my first week out of work was rolling over my 401K money from my former employer's plan into one of my other self-managed IRA accounts. Some people may not think this necessary, but I like having my money where I have control over it.

There may be an option to roll over old 401K funds into a plan with a new employer immediately, even though you may not be able to start contributing new funds to it for 3 to 6 months after your start date. If it's a good plan, by all means look at that option. Whatever you do, don't sit idly by and do nothing with that money. Many times, funds in old 401K plans end up sitting, forgotten about, not really earning anything. **Erin – rule number three: Don't let the 401K funds you had with your former employer sit dormant.** Unless the particular 401K plan you had with your former employer was out of this world, don't leave your money in it.

The last and most important thing I took care of was filing for unemployment. I knew I might be relying on these funds for some time. The whole experience with unemployment is guaranteed to make you feel really down on your luck, but **Erin – rule number four: Unemployment is a benefit you've earned, not a handout.** File for it expeditiously.

Hopefully, by the end of week one, all the loose ends from your former job will be tied up. Once you've finished making a clean and amicable break from your former employer, you'll be able to focus all of your time and energy on finding a new job.

Assuming you liked doing the kind of work you've been doing, the first place to begin a job search is within your network of industry friends and colleagues. For me, this meant people I'd known and worked with in the kitchen and bath industry- some for many years. Through these very same contacts, I'd landed my last four jobs.

Part of the work I do entails being actively involved in the National Kitchen and Bath Association. This is a group of like-minded professionals that holds monthly chapter meetings. Members are usually given educational lectures, as well as a chance to network with each other. I've made many friends over the years at these meetings. **Erin – rule number five: It's all about relationships; never discount or neglect professional networking.**

Your second week out of work should be spent beginning an organized, online job search. I stress 'organized' because job hunting, like any large project, is more effective when it's done efficiently.

You'll discover websites with job listings through word of mouth and exploring the internet. It won't take long to discern which resources are best for you and your particular circumstance.

For my job search, the websites I routinely looked at included: Craigslist.org, Indeed.com, Careerbuilder.com, Ctjobs.com, and the Waterbury-Republican classifieds.

Industry colleagues may also have a line on trade

specific sites you should check. In my case, I regularly scanned through the postings on: Ihireconstruction.com, Nkba.org, Woodweb.com and Woodjobs.com. I looked at the listings on all these sites a minimum of twice a week. I checked the ones that were the most user-friendly (like Craigslist.org) daily. It may sound like a lot of work; looking for employment is your new full-time job.

Job search portals are great because they help make you aware of available positions; however if you don't search multiple sites, you may not see all the job listings available to you.

I recently spoke to an industry headhunter about online job portals. He didn't hold out much hope for finding a job by utilizing them. He described how his e-mail address had accidently been inserted into a posting with which he was helping a client. Over the course of one weekend, he was e-mailed 1800 resumes'!

No company would have the manpower in their Human Resources department (if they even had one) to review that many resumes'. Knowing that doesn't mean you should cease to look for a job in this manner. **Erin-rule number six: Conduct your online search for a job as thoroughly and efficiently as possible, submitting as many resumes' as possible.** The law of averages will come into play; sooner or later your number will come up a winner. Let **everyone** know you're available and want to work.

My weekly job search schedule started early every Sunday morning. The first thing I did was scan through the new online job postings in Connecticut. This search took more than a couple of hours, but Sundays seemed to be the biggest day for new postings.

Another thing I'd accomplish on Sunday mornings was updating my employment status with Connecticut's automated unemployment system. This was a relatively painless process, which took only a few minutes because I fell within the normal parameters of the unemployed. I did it the hassle-free way, online.

Any employers who had posted jobs for which I felt I may be qualified would receive a copy of my resume' before the middle of that week. In today's job market, many prospective employers want to receive them online, never meeting you face to face. In fact, many go out of their way to remain anonymous and unreachable. This was unacceptable to me. If I thought a specific job was one I **really** wanted, I'd try to determine who the employer was and where they were located. Then I'd go there in person. **Erin – rule number seven: Find ways to stand out from the crowd of people all vying for the same position.** Getting 'face time' with a prospective employer shows initiative and, more importantly, gives you an opportunity to sell yourself.

During the week, I visited several places I'd sent resumes' to online. I'd show up unannounced, walk in and tell whoever was available that I wasn't sure if they'd received my resume' via e-mail, so I wanted to make certain they had a copy. In my mind, leaving a hard copy in person may possibly give a prospective employer an impression of me that couldn't be made via e-mail. More importantly, the visit allowed me to see the kind of facility in which a prospective employer's business was located. I won't work where the environment is shabby or people who walk through the door are treated like second-class citizens. Those things speak loudly about the quality of the company's management and/or ownership. If they don't care about these basics, how well do you think they treat their employees?

There may be times when you'll hear of a company and think it may be just the place for you to work. Perhaps their website further reinforces your opinion. **Erin – rule number eight: Don't ever base your opinion of a job or a workplace on a website alone.** Websites can be artfully deceptive. Recently I went looking for a specific millwork shop in New Haven. The 'facility' ended up being two row houses that were connected by an enclosed hallway and surrounded by razor wire, located in the absolute worse part of town. I never even went inside.

During the course of each workweek, I'd spend two or three days **literally** knocking on doors. First, I'd go online, decide on a specific geographic area I wanted to focus on that day and then do a search for companies that seemed promising in that area. After selecting five or six businesses, I'd establish a route, look up directions to all the stops and daisy chain them together. However long it took me to complete the entire run became the length of time I spent traveling that day.

Getting prepared for a physical job search was no different than getting ready for a typical workday. I'd take a shower and get dressed as if I was going off to work, visit the places on my list du jour and talk to anyone who'd listen. A fair amount of the time, I'd end up with some impromptu interviews, in part because people were impressed I was out pounding the pavement. I'd always leave a copy of my resume' and thank them for their time, even if I only got to see the receptionist.

For some people, knocking on doors in this manner may seem forward or outside their personal comfort zone. In a tough economic environment, you need to do whatever's necessary to find a job. You have to try and create your own opportunities where none seem to exist. Sitting around feeling sorry for your unemployed self is guaranteed to keep you unemployed. Suck it up, get out there and do it!

Knocking on doors will yield some rejection. Let the rejection roll off your back and keep going. Don't stop until you get a 'Yes'! Remember to keep a happy face, be positive, polite and personable.

I limited myself to no more then half a dozen cold calls a day. This formula gave me plenty of time for whatever conversations I'd end up having. It also allowed me to maintain a pleasant and positive attitude **without burning out**. After a day of knocking on doors, you'll discover how mentally challenging and tiring it can be. **Erin – rule number nine: Don't knock yourself out knocking on doors.**

People can sense negativity. You don't want to give off any negative vibes or appear to have low self-esteem in the presence of prospective employers. You want them to perceive you as a likable go-getter with qualities that would benefit their company, **not a 'Debbie Downer'.** First impressions are everything. If you begin to feel negative or beaten down during the course of any 'door knocking day', cut it short and use that time to do whatever it takes to get your head back on straight.

On that note, let's say you've planned a day of

knocking on doors and you wake up on the wrong side of the bed. Don't bother going out. Rearrange your schedule and use that day for quiet online research instead. It would be counter-productive to force yourself to be public and personable if you'd rather be alone. They say misery loves company. Well, don't try and bring potential employers on board with it. They're not interested.

Throughout your job search, never stop networking. Remember, out of sight, out of mind. Keep networking with everyone you know so they're aware you're still looking. You never know who may be listening or who may be in a position to help you find a new job. Don't be ashamed of any possible stigma attached to losing a job. Prospective employers understand economic downturns.

Saturday June 27, 2009 we were invited to a July 4th barbeque party at the home of one of your mom's colleagues. As you know, your mom has worked for the same company more than twenty-five years. You also know I used to work there as well, so many of her friends are people I know too.

I vacillated most of the day, Saturday, thinking of reasons why I shouldn't go. After a fair amount of prodding by your mom, I acquiesced and off we went.

In attendance at the barbeque were many high-powered people from your mom's company. One of them was the company's vice-president of distribution.

In a semi - confidential manner, he began explaining the tumultuous changes he was experiencing restructuring the company's national distribution and transportation system. He asked, "Have you ever thought about making a career change outside of the kitchen and bath industry?" I told him I'd already been sending out resumes' to businesses that were pushing the boundaries of my work experience.

He asked for a copy of my resume' and said he'd forward it to someone he knew who was a decision maker with one of the country's largest truck companies, a company that was looking for people like me from different walks of life, without formal trucking experience. They were in the process of trying to create an entirely new shipping model, one that would ultimately increase their profits.

I knew the odds of obtaining employment by having my resume' forwarded were slim, but I also knew the odds were better than those from making a cold call on a prospective employer. A door would essentially be opened for me, one through which many applicants off the street would never pass.

There are two reasons this opportunity came about: First of all, I'd always treated this gentleman and everyone else he knew in his company with respect; second, through my having networked with everyone I knew, he was aware of my situation. I hadn't 'whitewashed' it. While remaining upbeat and positive, I'd simply told everyone I knew about my lay-off and subsequent search for new employment. **Erin – rule number ten: Don't gloss over or lie about what's going on in your life with others.** It's all part of networking. You never know who may come through with a job lead for you.

If you find yourself unemployed, don't feel sorry for yourself and let negative thoughts bring you down even further. Get up, get dressed and get out in the world.

Take care of something around the house you've been avoiding. Take the dog out for a walk. Go and run some errands. Do anything to break up what may start feeling like a dull and monotonous routine.

You may begin to speculate about the potential end result of an impromptu interview with a prospective employer that goes well. **Erin – rule number eleven: Don't count your chickens before they hatch.** Don't waste a lot of time speculating and/or waiting on possible outcomes. Keep plugging away in your search until someone says 'You're hired'.

During week four of my job search, I did some research and contacted some of the local employment agencies specializing in people with my job skills. You'll discover, when conducting your research of employment agencies, they seem to specialize in certain fields.

I'm not a big proponent of employment agencies, but there are times when they may know about an opening not advertised elsewhere. A company looking to fill a position may hire them to screen applicants and find them qualified candidates. Make sure to tell the employment agency upfront you're only interested in fee paid positions; most, but not all, employment opportunities listed with agencies are fee paid.

In my tenth week out of work I expanded my job search to areas out of state. It wasn't a difficult decision. I wanted a job; I needed a paycheck. I started looking in Massachusetts, Rhode Island, Delaware, and parts of New York, Maryland and Virginia. If necessary, I decided I would rent a room for part of the week and then spend the balance of the week at home. These decisions were made jointly by your mother and me.

The end result of my comprehensive job search came when I recently started an exciting, new position with a kitchen and bath remodeling firm in Massachusetts. My industry networking and letters of recommendation paid off. An industry heavyweight I'd been in contact with forwarded my information to a dealer he knew with a growing business, in the process of opening a second showroom. There was a need for a project manager!

I started working at my new job on Monday, October 5th, 2009, after being out of work for fifteen weeks. It's an exciting, career broadening position with a company that has tremendous potential. I thank my lucky stars I never became discouraged in my job search. 2010 looks to be a very exciting year for me in my new career.

> *Erin,*
>
> *If you ever find yourself unemployed, remember it's not the lack of income that can be the most devastating, it's the effect on your mental state. Be organized, thorough and tireless in your job search and I guarantee you success. Oh, and make sure to be kind to yourself in the process.*
> *Love,*
> *Dad*

# Chapter 12   The Art of Selling Yourself

"Doing business without advertising is like winking at a girl in the dark. You know what you are doing, but nobody else does." Stuart Henderson Britt

*Dear Erin,*

*Selling yourself, or your product, to the world, is the most important aspect of your personal growth and success. Consider these situations: you find yourself in the position where it's necessary to market your abilities to an employer or perspective employer; you need to convince others your opinions and beliefs are valid; you become a salesperson whose success or failure is directly linked to how you present yourself and/or your product or service; or you want to win the heart of someone you love.*

*Life's all about selling. If you can't get anyone to listen to you and/or your ideas, much of success will be elusive. . . .*

Let me offer my essential rules for successful selling. I learned many of these techniques years ago when I started out as a door-to-door salesperson, literally knocking on doors each and every day. I can tell you from experience, if these rules are followed, they'll help you in dealing with whatever life throws your way.

**Perception is reality**. How others perceive you will become their reality, for better or worse. This means you must always strive to put your best foot forward so you're looked upon favorably. Others will view all your actions and make a determination about the kind of person you are, either consciously or sub-consciously. This, alone, is reason enough to remain aware of what you're doing, with whom you're doing it and how you're going about it.

It's said that in today's world there's a video camera at every corner. When you least expect it, you could end up being caught on film. Go about your life as though you were being taped 24/7; think before you speak and act. There's a saying, 'Life is a stage.' Well it really is and your audience is comprised of people you see and deal with in your day-to-day life, your family and friends in particular.

**Persistence wears down resistance.** Some people, including salespeople, think of 'persistence' negatively, as being pushy or obnoxious and that's not how you should treat someone. This almost always brings to mind a vision of the door-to-door vacuum cleaner salesman (which I was at one time), their foot in the door, trying to coerce inno-cent 'victims' into buying something they don't need. Per-sistence doesn't need to be over the top and rude. If used properly, it can be a valuable tool. I like to call it being 'pleasantly and positively persistent', or PPP.

PPP can be used to successfully persuade another person (or persons) that your way of thinking is the right way. It can effectively work to get a response from someone (like an employer) when they might not otherwise want to respond. It can also be utilized to motivate others to do something. I often use this technique until I get the response I want. For example, I may want to know when someone's cabinetry will be produced and ready to ship. A particular vendor may be hemming and hawing at committing to a date. I'll be pleasantly and positively persistent until I get an answer.

It can be difficult, at times, not to cross the line from PPP to becoming just plain pushy-JPP. Try and keep your dealings polite enough so that won't happen, but make sure you get your point across. Make certain it's understood why you're not backing off. If the other party clearly understands why you're persevering, it'll keep the exchange from becoming confrontational.

There will be times where you'll literally want to stick your foot in the door and be more aggressive in your persistent stance. You may feel like you're so close to a breakthrough, you can't fold up your tent. Be advised, when it gets to this point, it's treacherous to continue pushing. You'll most certainly create an 'all or nothing proposition', versus perhaps winning some smaller, but worthwhile battle. Pay attention and decide whether it's worth pushing and, if so, how hard.

Whatever else you do, try and make sure there are no hard feelings in the end. Don't be afraid to apologize, explaining why you needed to go to the extent you did. This has worked for me on many occasions after I've verbally cornered someone in an effort to get an answer and held my ground. Many of my 'victims' are still my friends despite my harsh treatment. My apologies and explanations were heartfelt enough to make them understand the situation in which I found myself.

**Don't sell the steak; sell the sizzle.** Many salespeople don't seem to be able to distinguish themselves from their rivals. Selling similar products or services, they end up becoming a face in the crowd, which leaves them only one avenue of competition: a pricing war with countless others. With few exceptions, the outcome remains the same; the lowest bid wins. All the salesmanship in the world can't help you change the outcome of that foot race.

Selling the 'sizzle' of your product is how you distinguish yourself from the others. Remember Erin, being average is boring and totally unmemorable. Think about when we're watching 'American Idol'. When one of the contestants gets up in front of the world and just goes through the motions, what does Simon say? He tells them this is a competition to see who the best singer in the world is. There's no room for run of the mill.

Whether a material thing, a service, or you as a person, the same principle applies. Concentrate on your qualities and/or the features of your product and how they'll benefit the buyer. Establish value in their mind. Here again, perception is reality.

In order to remain a step ahead of your competitors, you must first select the market niche on which you want to focus. Remember, it's impossible to be all things to all people. Once you figure out what you're especially good at, you can start defining your place in the market and/or the world.

Once you've established what your bailiwick is, work at being the very best in your field. Identify your target demographic. Promote your strong points and create a marketing campaign built around them. This holds true in promoting anything: you, your personal skills, or your product.

From a client's or employer's perspective, they want to know **why** they should buy something from **you**. What's special about your product or service? What makes it stand out from the rest? Be ready to run down a list of ways you and/or your product will benefit them.

**People are not buying your product; they're buying you.** Most sales are made because you manage to win the heart of your client in some way, whether they simply decide they like you or you somehow click with them by instilling confidence and respect, **your product is secondary**. Regardless of whether it's a five dollar item or a half million dollar house, the deciding factor in most cases is **you**. Work on developing a relationship with your client.

Understanding the importance of relationships with customers and other people is what separates the truly successful salesperson from the clerk or order taker. They'll cultivate their relationships with their clients and, in this manner, gain enough trust to build a referral base. There's an old saying, "The top 20 percent of salespeople account for 80 percent of the business." The biggest reason for this is because of a salesperson's likeability and networking skills with clients, colleagues and friends alike. Never forget, it's all about relationships. You may have to set some limits, but you need to get along with other people in order to get along in business and life.

**Talk to lots of people.** What good is it to believe in yourself and your ideas if no one else knows about you or them? This rule is often overlooked. The more opportunities you make for yourself to get out and pitch yourself and/or your product, the more the likelihood you'll find success.

Some salespeople get complacent at times. Maybe they've been swamped with work and had some recent successes, requiring exhausting amounts of time and effort. They decide it's okay to take a step back and relax. This practice is referred to as 'resting on one's laurels'. It amounts to committing suicide if you're a salesperson, yet I've seen it and continue to see it done all the time.

You should **never** take any sales success for granted. Don't stop creating new opportunities for yourself. Keep making the effort and putting yourself out there on stage everyday to achieve continued success in your life.

**Don't talk your way past the sale.** This is one of the biggest mistakes salespeople consistently make. You have to learn when to shut your mouth. This means you need to be engaged with the other person and listening to what they're saying. It also means it cannot be all about 'you-you-you'. If they want to talk about themselves, let them, and act as if you're interested in what they have to say.

The very instant they offer any kind of buying signal, stop talking and let them make the purchase. There will be plenty of other opportunities to speak with them about whatever they like later. Close the sale!

Making a purchase is properly defined as signing the paperwork and getting the money. Until you get the cash, it's not a sale, only a very optimistic prospect. Remember not to count on anything based solely upon someone's word. The deal is only closed when you've got the cash in hand.

**Be able to accept rejection and not take it personally.** The hardest aspect of selling is in dealing with rejection. Constantly being told 'no' can have negative psychological effects if you let the rejection get to you. You may start questioning yourself and your abilities. It could even start to make you second guess other things about you as a person.

The reality is, throughout your life you'll hear 'no' much more often than 'yes'. From loved ones, to friends, to employers, to perspective clients, it can start sounding like a recording, 'No! No! No!'

When I worked as a sales trainer, back in my door-to-door vacuum cleaner sales days, I was aware of the devastating effects constantly hearing 'no' could have on a salesperson. We had a formula, which was continually pounded into the heads of all the new people we hired: If, during the course of any given year, they spoke with 14,000 people and only 250 said 'yes' they'd earn a minimum of $25,000 a year. If they followed that formula, we assured them they'd be successful.

Back in the mid-seventies, that was decent money for a lot of the guys. We'd tell them 'a minimum income of $25,000' because invariably they'd earn more from other residual sales along the way, primarily through sales to people who needed parts for their existing machines (bags, belts, replacement attachments, miscellaneous repairs, etc.). Our salesmen were paid a commission on anything they sold.

The point is, the same holds true with many things in life. I'm currently going out knocking on doors looking for a new job. It's tough to hear 'no, we aren't hiring' over and over. But I only need one yes and I'll be all set. The goal of getting a job helps me ignore the negatives and remain hopeful and positive that soon I'll get the yes for which I'm looking.

**You can only sell what you believe in.** It's impossible to successfully represent something (be it yourself, or a product or service) with conviction unless you're a believer. This is true with anything in life. If you don't believe in your boss or the company you work for, how can you represent them? If you don't believe in your significant other, how can you build a life together with them? If you don't believe how great your product or service is how can you sell it to the public at large? How can you sell your abilities to someone if you doubt yourself?

You cannot have success, or a fulfilling life, if you don't believe in yourself, your abilities and what you're doing. If you find yourself in this position, make the changes necessary to feel proud of yourself as a person and also the things you do. You have to like what you see when you look in the mirror.

**The sale is made in your head first.** One technique that's used by successful salespeople is to visualize a closing before the presentation is actually made. In fact, they'll create the scene of a contract signing and play it over and over again in their heads, preparing for the actual event. This comprehensive, positive, mental preparation then becomes a self-fulfilling prophecy.

Instead of using this positive approach, some sales-people go into a presentation doubting its outcome beforehand. They start to worry about the price they need to present to their client and how it may measure up to that of other possible competitors. This leads to second guessing their product, their strategy and the sale's outcome. Forget all of that! Don't over analyze the negative outcomes there could conceivably be.

Let your clients determine whether you have what they need. Ultimately you can't control what they think, so why worry too much about it? Focus on the things you can control. Are you giving them the most comprehensive presentation? Have you made the product's value apparent? Are you being yourself? Based on what you've discussed in your meetings with them, do you have the right solution? Now with all that in place, picture yourself successfully closing the sale.

**Develop a sense of empathy.** When relating to other people, it's not only important to speak well, but to have even better listening skills. Empathy is the ability to look at things from another person's position. It means making yourself secondary to another's wants or needs. You must be able to understand where the other person is coming from and genuinely care about their situation.

Being empathetic is largely overlooked in today's world. People spend more time concentrating on their own needs and not concerning themselves with the needs of others. This selfish attitude permeates all aspects of our lives.

The truly successful salesperson understands the importance of their client's feelings and concerns. They understand the need to be viewed as a caring and compassionate person. If other people sense these qualities within you, they'll be much more comfortable offering up their faith and trust to you.

**Learn How to Smile.** The power of a warm, friendly smile is immeasurable. As a rule people will do an instant assessment of you as a person within the first few seconds of meeting you. Listen to me again- within seconds! They'll decide if they like you, or not. Will they choose to open the door and invite you in as a guest, or not? Are you nice, or not? Once this decision is rendered in their mind, it's **extremely** difficult to change. The best single way of increasing your likeability during this initial assessment process, is by smiling.

A heartfelt smile is more of an icebreaker between you and another person than anything else. It sets a pleasant and positive tone to any meeting. You'll appear to be more friendly, confident and trustworthy. It will elicit a warm and positive response from the other person in return; they'll instantly feel more at ease.

Even when preparing to speak on the phone, it's advisable to smile before picking up the receiver. If you put a small mirror near the phone with a note reminding you to smile, it will help you remember and you'll literally sound more pleasant to the party on the other end. To this day when I'm having a bad day before picking up the phone, I'll make myself smile.

**Control the sale.** All too often, many so-called salespeople are nothing more than glorified order takers. Their sales technique is little more than taking out a pen and paper and making notes on what their client wants. They then take that list and process it, verbatim. Acting as the court stenographer is not selling. If this is what your sales technique has turned into, either look at ways of improving it, or change careers.

Selling, as an art, involves listening to what the client believes they want and, through your expertise and knowledge, pointing them towards where they really should be heading. When all the variables are properly addressed, everyone winds up happy: the client with the product or service they've purchased and you with the closed sale. The two of you may even wind up friends.

If you allow your perspective clients to run rough shod over you and your ideas, it'll usually end up unfavorably for at least one of you. More often than not, both parties involved in a poorly executed sale come out of it unhappy: the salesperson is left feeling as if they didn't do their best; and the client feels like they didn't get their money's worth. Chances of future sales opportunities with that client become non-existent.

A poorly crafted sale has other long lasting effects as well. The clients of these sales are unlikely to refer you, as a salesperson, to their friends. They probably won't recommend your company at all, as you are a reflection of said company. In fact, if you do a poor enough job, they'll take every opportunity to bad-mouth you, your company and the product/services you sell. If this happens with any kind of regularity, the effects on your business and your reputation will be catastrophic. Negative press of this variety can spread like wild fire, severely hampering you in future dealings.

**Honesty is still the best policy.** In spite of the best efforts of some people to the contrary, **you** need to be honest with people. Fast-talking and trying to pull one over on someone may allow you to achieve some short-term gain, but it's extremely short-lived.

As I'm writing this today, the Wall Street figure responsible for the largest Ponzi scheme ever, Bernie Madoff, was convicted of fraud. He'd been lying to investors for years, bilking them out of billions of dollars. The judge showed no mercy and sentenced him to 150 years in jail. How great do you think old Bernie thinks his boats and houses are now?

One of my favorite singers/songwriters, Don Henley, wrote and sings a song, 'The Garden of Allah'. There's a line in the song, 'There are no truths, there is no lies-just data to be manipulated'. Quite a cynical view to have about life, but I have to say I'm in total agreement. There seems to be an overabundance of people that live and act as if that quote is an acceptable state of affairs. Don't aim to be another immoral, empty suit with no sense of right or wrong.

I've often shared stories of my door-to-door sales experiences with others. One of the things they find fascinating is that our sales 'bible' was Dr. Seuss's, 'Green Eggs and Ham'. We used to order copies of the book by the case. It was assigned reading to all our new salespeople. If you take the time to read this book, it encapsulates the sales process in a way anyone can understand. I would recommend everyone get a copy and read it.

. . . *Erin, please make sure you memorize these essential rules for selling and living. You'll find great use for these techniques in all aspects of your life. They may be the greatest gift I can ever give you.*

*Love,*

*Dad*

## Chapter 13    Credit & Investment

"A penny here and a dollar there, placed at interest, goes on accumulating, and in this way the desired result is attained.  It requires some training, perhaps, to accomplish this economy, but when once used to it, you will find there is more satisfaction in rational saving than in irrational spending."  P.T. Barnum

*Dear Erin,*
*You'll find, as you set out on your path through*
*life, one of the most difficult challenges before you*
*will be managing your finances well.  Saving*
*money, trying to get ahead, can prove to be quite*
*tricky.  It'll take a considerable amount of under-*
*standing, planning, commitment and discipline to*
*become financially successful. . . .*

## WASTEFUL SPENDING

Money isn't something you should ever take for granted. You need to fully appreciate its influence: it can be positive, if you respect it, and personally devastating, if you waste it.

When you first start out on your own, you'll invariably end up wasting lots of money, mostly because it'll seem like there are so many things you need and so many others you want. You'll feel like you need to jump right in and start checking things off your list. Many young people end up in a quagmire of debt because they try to live beyond their means. One of my goals is to keep this from happening to you.

The most important thing for you to realize is that you don't need to buy everything **now**. In fact, much of what you **think** you need will end up collecting dust or being disposed of in the future. Try and temper your urges to spend money in an effort to acquire things.

Spending money will be part of fully experiencing and appreciating your new and exciting independent lifestyle. Be aware that going out for drinks with friends to a club can burn up a lot of cash if you do it every Friday night, but so can stopping for a latte before work every weekday morning. Activities like these can be a real drain on your already limited finances.

If you and your friends can come up with inexpensive ways to enjoy each other socially, I'd highly recommend it. The bar scene ends up getting played out pretty quickly. Having a bunch of friends over for pizza, to watch a movie, or for game night is much more fun and far less expensive.

The answer for many young people seems simple enough: earn more money. The problem is the pace at which your income increases will most certainly be slower than the rate you continue to spend. Even if you get extremely lucky career-wise, it won't ever be enough to mitigate the constant financial shortfall in which you'll find yourself. As a rule, the more you make, the more you'll spend and, at the beginning of your young adult life, the equation won't ever balance.

At some point your spending spree will need to stop and you'll have to get serious about money. You'll need to begin thinking about budgeting. The reasons could be any or all of these: maybe you'll drive yourself into so much debt you simply can't spend anymore; you could decide you want to purchase a new car or buy a home; perhaps you'll meet someone and decide it's time to build a life together; or possibly you'll just get tired of being on the hamster wheel, earning more just so you can spend more.

Whatever the reason, you'll finally decide to stop uncontrolled spending. Assuming that point in time is now, if you're to be any kind of a financial success with your life, there are some basic rules you need to follow:

### PAY YOURSELF FIRST

When I was growing up, my dad drummed this into my head. I didn't listen and never completely grasped the concept. Pay attention here. This is the most important part of your financial wellbeing: **If there is no reward in it for you directly, what's the point?**

Paying yourself first will mean different things at different stages of your life. Starting out on your own, it will probably mean you do nothing more than save a little money every week - putting something away for a rainy day. If you're able to accomplish this, you're among a select few of your peers and my hat's off to you.

For your mother and me, we have different goals and reasons for paying ourselves first. We need to make sure we have some money put away so when things like my recent lay-off occur, we can weather the storm. We also have to think about our retirement; most of our current savings is for that.

Whatever your financial state, regardless of the circumstances and influences you face, **always be sure to pay yourself firs**t. Even if it hurts-do it!

### Start a Retirement Plan

This is another one of those rules many young people like to ignore. With all the uncertainty in today's world, it's important you start to put away something for your retirement **now**. Don't procrastinate! I don't care if you're fresh out of college and broke. It's the second most important thing to work on for your financial security and it's important you begin **now**. Even a small IRA account is a step in the right direction. Get in the habit of regularly, whether it's weekly or monthly, saving for your golden years.

The most popular and painless way to save for your retirement will probably be by participating in a 401K Plan (offered by private employers) or a 403B Plan (offered to public sector employees). Virtually every employer has one of these in place. These are plans where you put money aside for your retirement.

If your employer has such a plan, you want to start contributing to it A.S.A.P. You also want to put aside as much as you can. The longer you contribute money and have that money working for you earning more money, the larger the nest egg you'll accumulate.

The great thing with 401K plans is that the money you contribute gets deducted from your paycheck before any taxes get taken out. I don't know if you can appreciate this, but you don't want to give the government any more money than is required by law. You also want to make sure you contribute enough to collect the maximum matching contribution the company you work for may offer.

Some companies offer a 401K 'match' payment that is usually a percentage of what you contribute, up to a certain dollar amount or 'cap'. For example, company A may match your contributions at the rate of 25% to a maximum of $1500.00. Make sure, at the very least, you are contributing enough to your 401K to get the maximum match. If you don't do this, you're essentially leaving your money on the table, giving back to the company – not too smart.

### BUYING A HOUSE

A home is the biggest single investment you'll probably make in your lifetime. The amount of money involved can be staggering. You need to be adequately prepared before making such a life changing decision and purchase.

Let me begin by saying if you can't afford it, **wait**. You shouldn't be considering the purchase of a home until you've legitimately saved enough money for a down payment and you can qualify for a standard, fixed-rate mortgage.

In order to buy a home in the traditional context today, you'll probably be required to come up with a minimum of a twenty percent down payment. A twenty percent requirement is standard for most banks granting mortgages. It's an amount reflective of serious commitment, leaving the bank feeling confident you won't default on your long-term financial responsibility.

If you want to get a mortgage with less than a standard down payment, you'll need to pay something called Private Mortgage Insurance, or PMI. PMI guarantees the bank they'll get paid if you default on your mortgage. This is a monthly payment amount that gets added onto your mortgage payment. Once a mortgage is set up with PMI, it's usually a minimum of five years before you can have it removed.

As far as I'm concerned, PMI is a complete waste of money, much the same as paying interest on a credit card. You're better off waiting until you can meet the requirements of a standard mortgage to buy a home.

Once you've saved funds for a down payment on a house, I'd highly recommend you meet with a qualified mortgage broker to determine how much you can **safely** spend. They'll take all aspects of your financial profile into consideration: your income, how much debt you have, what kind of debt it is, etc. Make sure they understand you want a **standard mortgage**, which in most cases will be a thirty-year, fixed-rate loan.

Don't get involved with any financial wizard types who promise they can get you more money than anyone else. You've heard the saying, 'if it sounds too good to be true, then it probably is?' Well, that's right! Look at all the people in trouble today because so many phony baloney 'exotic' mortgages were granted! There may be exceptions to my rule, but I'm only looking at conservative and safe ways for you to help secure your future financial status.

Once you've determined how much of a mortgage you're qualified for and you have your down payment funds in place, you can start looking for your dream house. It's important to take your time and be thorough in your search. There is a lot of sub-standard housing for sale. Ask yourself, if a house is truly great why would the people living in it be selling it? Why has it been on the market for 6 months? Granted there are some extenuating circumstances (i.e. divorce, relocation, etc.), but I would recommend maintaining a skeptical view when looking to buy any house.

Understand many, if not most, states are still 'buyer beware' when it comes to real estate purchases. This means **you** carry the burden of risk, not the seller. You're responsible, even if you don't realize you're buying a lemon. I've known a few people over the years that have gotten burned badly on real estate deals.

You may quickly discover you don't like any of the houses you've looked at in the price range you can afford. If that's the case, wait. I wouldn't recommend settling for a house you really don't like just because it's affordable. It can put undo strain on a relationship, not to mention your own mental and emotional wellbeing. Going home at night after a hard day at work should be soothing, not the worst part of your day.

Overextending yourself financially to buy a house is a recipe for disaster. You'll end up using funds you may potentially need for other things, necessitating the borrowing of even more money.

## THE GOOD AND BAD OF CREDIT

In today's world, there may be times when borrowing money becomes a necessary evil. Most large purchases, such as a new car or a house, are done with some borrowed funds. It's comfortable to know you can borrow money if needed, but the less frequently you go 'to the till', the better off you'll be. Never abuse credit privileges.

Many people end up borrowing money on a regular basis, in order to make ends meet. They start overextending themselves by living beyond their means and depending on credit cards. In the short term, it feels good to have access to easy money. Buying whatever you want, whenever you want it, and not having to worry about paying for it right away can give you a false sense of satisfaction.

The use of credit cards can be a slowly tightening noose around your neck. As the balances owed begin to grow, so do the minimum payments you'll be required to make. The interest credit card companies charge you for the loan (that is what an unpaid balance is) also continues to grow.

It can become quite disheartening when you owe thousands of dollars; making minimum payments isn't enough to keep the balances from growing larger. It's like swimming against the tide. You can't get anywhere. God forbid you miss a credit card payment's due date. The penalty fees attached are onerous and get tacked onto your unpaid balance with ever more interest.

Some people get sucked into a slow credit spiral downward and have to resort to obtaining more credit cards, using them to try and make ends meet. They start charging the monthly payments due on the older cards with the higher balances to newer cards with the lower balances. Individual balances grow, while cumulative debt soars. There are more people than you can imagine drowning in debt, trying to maintain the minimum payments required on all their credit cards.

Something else I want to mention: you don't need a whole array of credit cards in order to function in society. I have heard it said the average consumer has 8 different credit cards. I've been functioning with three for several years now. In fact, I would only have one if I could get away with it, my American Express card.

I don't want this to be perceived as an ad for the American Express card, but I love my American Express card because it's not a credit card. It's a charge card. The difference is a charge card enables you to make a purchase but it also means when you receive your monthly statement **you're expected to pay the entire amount owed**. Some argue, what's the point of having a charge card then? For me, it's a way of defraying expenses for a few weeks, if needed. It also governs me because I can't run up an unpaid balance. I'm required to pay it off when I get my monthly statement.

Some merchants won't accept an American Express card, which is one of the reasons I also have a Master-

Card. I set my card limit on this one at $500.00 and never maintain any kind of an open balance on it. It lives in my wallet to give me an emergency source of money if I need it and that's all.

The only other credit card I hold is from Macy's. Your mom and I like the clothing they carry. The only time I ever use it is when I'm Christmas shopping for you and her. I'll go in and spend a few hundred dollars within short order and then pay off the balance in January.

Let's talk more about conservative financial practices from which you'd benefit:

**One absolute financial no-no is taking equity out of your house whenever the need for cash arises.** Until recently, some people did this routinely, under the false assumption home values would forever increase. Your home should be treated as if it were a savings account with a variable return. Even during times where it isn't appreciating in value, you're still putting money away by paying down your mortgage. It will always hold some value. You may need your home's equity for something truly significant down the road such as your retirement, or helping your kids with college tuition. In fact, for many people the equity in their home is a sizable part of their retirement portfolio.

The recent economic meltdown from which the country is recovering is proof of what a fool's game it was to believe home values couldn't ever decline. There are so many people who owe considerably more on mortgages and equity loans than what their house is worth in today's housing market. Many have chosen to simply walk away and let the banks foreclose.

The second biggest expense faced by many people is the purchase of a car. I like driving a nice car as much as the next guy, but I never lose sight of its main purpose - to get me from point A to point B, reliably and in relative comfort.

Over the years the car industry has done its darnedest to make their products not only desirable, but the types of status symbols people sometimes pay exorbitant amounts of money to own. You know, "Be the first on your block to own one of our latest rolling works of art!" Expensive cars cost more to buy, more to insure, more to maintain and more to repair. The financial drain never ends.

I'll admit, when I was younger I wanted to own the coolest car. It was only after abusing many cars and realizing the cost and inconvenience involved, that my practical side took over. I'm now more of the 'point A to point B' ilk. In fact, I don't like putting my cars out to pasture even when the time comes where I should. Erin, look how much we both like my old truck! We have more fun riding around in that then we ever would in the latest model, fully loaded Porsche.

The way to buy a car is to look for something you like. Make sure it's comfortable, fun to drive, reasonably economical and within your budgetary means. Plan on taking care of it and driving it until the wheels fall off.

Overall it's important to try and be conservative in your spending habits. One way of controlling how much money you spend is budgeting. People have different methods of doing this. Your mom uses a spread sheet set up in her computer. Other people will go out and buy a formal bookkeeping system like Quicken. There are also people who use the old school, envelope method. I don't care which technique you use as long as you get into the habit of watching your money.

Part of a budget is earmarking funds for everything, including savings. If you're lucky enough, you'll find yourself in a position where you can save a lot of money for different things. Maybe you have a Christmas club account, college education fund for the kids, a vacation fund, rainy day fund and retirement savings. Maybe you have a hobby or want to continue your own education. Your individual circumstances will dictate how much you can save for what. Again, the important thing is to get into the habit of doing it.

Some of what you save will be relatively painless. All you need to do is have it taken out of your paycheck so you never end up with the money in your pocket. Some companies will let you set up payroll deductions for a variety of things. Most will provide a 401K plan that we mentioned earlier. You may be able to have money diverted directly into a savings account as well. Your mom currently has money being deducted and put into three different accounts.

I find automatic deposit and payroll deduction great ways to limit your spending. I'm the kind of person who really has to pay attention to the amount of money I'm spending. I do everything in my power to make sure I don't ever have any on my person. For example, I purposely don't have an ATM card or any way of getting cash advances on my credit card. If I need money, I have to go to the trouble of having your mom get me some, or physically going to the bank and cashing a check. If you find you're like me, make your access to cash as difficult as possible.

. . .*Erin, there's a lot more involved in investment and credit than what I've covered here. There's so much involved that it would take an entire book devoted to the subject to go into any kind of detail at all about the different types of investments available and understanding how they work. I'm planning to write that book. It'll be based on what I've learned about investing and what I've successfully accomplished with my money.*
*Let's assume you're a fiscally responsible adult and you've followed some of my advice. You're now a little older and have accumulated an investment portfolio for yourself. Good for you!! Hopefully, it's diversified: a portion of it being equity built up in the value of your home; a substantial 401K account you've been contributing to for several years; some stock; and certificates of deposit as a result of having saved a little money every week for a rainy day. It's all good and it all counts.*
*If you reach this stage financially and have no debt, as far as I am concerned you're a raging success. That doesn't mean you should rest on your laurels and relax. You always need to be vigilant concerning your financial state of affairs.*
*Love,*
*Dad*

# Chapter 14  Time Management

"We all sorely complain of the shortness of time, and yet have much more than we know what to do with. Our lives are either spent in doing nothing at all, or in doing nothing to the purpose, or in doing nothing that we ought to do. We are always complaining that our days are few and acting as though there would be no end of them."  Lucius Annaeus Seneca

*Dearest Erin,*
*I've been told on numerous occasions over the*
*years how well I manage my time.  I want to im-*
*part some of my methodology on you with the*
*hope that you, in turn, will become proficient at it.*
*Making good use of your time will be beneficial in*
*helping you lead a more fulfilling life. . . .*

Effective time management is contingent on the mastery of three co-dependent aspects:

Prioritizing tasks that require your personal attention.

Efficient and realistic budgeting of your time.

Task completion in a timely manner.

Failure to perform any one of these well, will have a direct negative impact on the remaining two.

The first thing people often notice when dealing with me is my punctuality. No matter what, I'm almost always on time or early. When I'm late, there's an awfully good reason and I let people waiting on me know as soon as I can - preferably prior to my arrival. This way they can make whatever adjustments are necessary to their schedules.

Being punctual is one of the most important aspects of personal time management. It shows others you value their time as important and you're someone who does what they say they'll do. (Nobody likes to wait for anything - especially someone who's late.) Punctuality also gets whatever schedule you've created for yourself started out on the right foot.

Some people you'll meet and/or have dealings with will feel that making a concerted effort to be on time all the time is some kind of personal problem. But Erin, these are the very same people that are often late and disorganized. Habitually tardy people are usually arrogant, believing their time is more important than the time of others.

There's nothing wrong with striving to **always** be on time. Look at it this way: If you start out trying to be a bit early and you miss the mark, at minimum you'll end up being prompt most of the time. What helps you to consistently accomplish this feat is budgeting your time properly.

Just as you should pay yourself first when it comes to your finances, part of budgeting your time includes allowing some time every day to do the things you want to do before filling up the rest of it with other people's wants and needs. Oh, and 'other people' would include family. Pick a part of the day where you feel fresh and are able to look at things objectively and positively. Don't try to make time for yourself after others have brutalized you all day long. You'll only end up short-changing yourself.

Erin, as you're aware, I'm an early riser. Usually I'm up and about at around 4:00 A.M. This gives me at least an hour of uninterrupted time where I can ease my way into the day, doing things I enjoy. These activities include having the news on in the background while I check my e-mail and look in on a couple blogs I follow.

As you know, one of my fascinations is the stock market. Being considered an active trader, I find all the happenings of the financial world intriguing. Once I catch up on the news of the day, the T.V. gets switched to the Bloomberg channel. I can see what happened overnight in Asia and check the stock futures. This plays in the background while I access various investor message boards online; searching for tidbits of information on stocks I own and/or am considering buying.

Just as some people forget to take care of their health and others neglect to pay themselves first, still others don't make time for the things they enjoy. Let me give you an example.

My friend, Jenn, is one of the most lovable and personable people on earth. Extremely career driven, she spends inordinate amounts of time working late nights and weekends. Often these work binges leave her completely drained and stressed, not feeling good about much of anything. I hate to see her like that; she's just not well-equipped for it. The most exasperating aspect of it for me is how she leaves no time in her schedule to pursue her painting.

Jenn is a tremendously gifted painter. Her chosen medium is watercolor, although I'm certain she'd have no trouble adjusting to others if she so chose. We have some of her paintings on display in our home and have had many friends admire them, wanting to know where they could see more.

On occasion, when Jenn's been frustrated, she's expressed her desire to have more time for herself. I've offered my sympathy and advice to no avail. She remains career driven, sacrificing her true wellbeing along the way.

To help Jenn break her endless cycle of career pursuit and subsequent stress, I've offered a potential solution to her. In fact, I've recommended the same process to others who've found themselves in Jenn's position. My technique has been successful for each of them when they adhere to it.

Anyone who finds they don't have any time for themselves should take out their calendar and begin making appointments **for themselves.** Look ahead two or three months and block out a day as if it were an appointment with a client. The key is to keep the appointment and not let anyone or anything steal that time back from you. It doesn't matter how the calendar entry is labeled – as long as you use that time for yourself. For example, Jenn likes to paint. She could start blocking out every Monday and label it 'Attend watercolor seminar'. It's just that easy.

Proper prioritization of tasks is also critical to good time management. Making time for all the things important to you can occasionally seem very daunting. Some days, it'll feel like everyone, everywhere needs you **now**. I remember reading somewhere, 'Improper scheduling on your part doesn't necessarily constitute an emergency on mine.' Try and not let too many other people's 'emergencies' botch up your schedule.

Erin, let's assume you have your priorities straight and that you've taken the time for yourself that you need. Now you can get on with the rest of it. Prioritizing tasks is similar to setting goals. You may need to write them down – one complete list or, depending on what you have going on, several. Don't rely on your memory, unless you have a very short agenda.

A written list will help you sort through and evaluate all the things that appear to require your immediate attention. Pay attention to what I'm saying: things that **appear** to need your attention. Once you start this kind of evaluation, I guarantee you'll find many of the items on your list hardly matter. They can either wait, or be eliminated altogether.

Once your priorities are down on paper and in order, you can start working on them, picking them off, one by one. Remember to use a rifle - not a shotgun. Avoid being needlessly sidetracked by any lesser tasks, lower down your list. Think about and take care of one thing at a time, before moving on to the next. Try not to get caught up in ancillary side issues that would take you away from the task at hand. Don't hesitate to just say 'no' if a matter isn't high on your priority list, or if it's something that can wait until a better time. Long-term priorities usually aren't as important as the shorter-term '911s'; however, all should be reviewed on a regular basis so nothing is neglected. But remember, first things first.

Realistic scheduling is the key part of good time management that seems to be the hardest element to master. Many people have the most trouble here, the main reason being most of us don't truly keep track of all the things requiring our time. Personal appointment books I've seen over the years often contain only the most cryptic of entries. While some people may be perfectly fine functioning this way, it isn't enough for most people to stay organized. Be as specific and detailed in your calendar and list(s) of priorities as possible.

One way to manage your schedule is by calculating the required time needed for each task or event involved. Try working from the end back to the beginning (at least that's how I do it) when calculating how much time is needed. Include adequate time for each and every single step. **Make sure you include any travel time both ways.** The end could mean the end of the day, the end of the week, or the end of a specific project. Be sure that as you make each time calculation, you build in small 'buffers'.

Buffers are small blocks of time that get added into your schedule (a.k.a. fudge factor). Invariably they'll end up being used to cover any unforeseen delays, or unexpected minor crises that may arise along the way. An example of this would be calculating how much time you need to get to a client's home for a meeting. In ideal conditions, it may be a twenty-minute drive, but I'd probably budget twenty-five to be safe. If you arrive a couple minutes early, you have a much more manageable situation than if you get there late.

I have a friend who likes to tell everyone how well 'she works to a deadline'. The truth is, she can't remain focused enough to plan out her time properly. Too many things are allowed to creep into the picture causing distractions, eating up her time and forcing her to work under pressure to meet her deadlines. Strive to limit your distractions so you can remain on task and you'll accomplish much more, with less stress.

I like to structure my schedule so I end up with large blocks of 'free' time, as opposed to having an hour free here and a half hour there. I'm able to accomplish more, in a less interrupted fashion, than if my schedule was peppered with smaller blocks of 'free' time throughout the day. Even though I'm very regimented in my personal scheduling, I end up **appearing** to be more flexible than many people, because I may just happen to have one of these blocks of 'free' time available when it's most needed.

When I was a salesperson, I would try and make client appointments early (on the way in) or late in the day (on the way home)–not in the middle day. I found it to be more disruptive if I made appointments in the middle of the day because they may not start on time, or they could run late – potentially screwing up my daily schedule on both ends. Clients were usually accepting of my early/late arrangement for the same reason -it was less disruptive on their schedule as well. I recommend that you offer people choices from you're planned availability. This way, they still have options, but they're limited to times that work best for you. That's a win-win situation.

If you end up being a person in demand, who's needed in too many places through the course of the day or week, more entries may need to be made in your schedule. I wrote earlier about calculating the time you need by figuring how much is necessary for each individual step of a task or project. You may need to literally list out each individual part of your day in this manner. For example, 10:00-10:15 A.M. – coffee and check e-mail. 10:15-11:20 A.M. – Prepare for staff meeting. 11:20-11:45 – grab a bite to eat. Be as specific as you can, so when you find yourself in overwhelming schedule situations, you'll have a clearer picture of your predicament. Those extra entries will take a little time to make, but may call attention to a looming conflict, allowing you to make more gradual transitions accordingly. Making accurate and detailed entries will end up paying for themselves.

A scheduling concern for us all is **time for family**. One way people deal with scheduling conflicts is to dip into their day off, Sundays, or any other time they've set aside for themselves. I frown on this practice. It's extremely important to have time away from work and share time with your family: going on vacation, attending your kids' soccer game, quiet time with your spouse, etc. Adequate family time should be scheduled, no matter what. If you feel scheduling constraints trapping you, look at your calendar for the following month and schedule your family time. Make it the first entry every week right after the block of time you left for yourself. Again, don't allow anything or anybody else to steal these scheduled blocks of time back from you.

When it comes to time management, task completion is more important than you'd think. I'm sure you know that miscellaneous odds and ends can really get in the way of your productivity. If you allow this to happen, the more important tasks requiring your attention might sit unfinished, spiraling out of control and causing you to miss critical target dates. The following are some methods I use to try and keep this annoyance to a minimum:

1. Establish when you're at your best mentally and tackle your complex responsibilities, beginning with the ones you dislike most. Personally, if I can finish a complex task or one I dislike, it gives me a mental boost and makes the rest of the day much easier.

2. Don't forget about focus. Concentration is a necessary part of task completion. As I've already mentioned, learn to use a rifle not a shotgun. Work on one thing at a time, before moving on to the next.

> . . . *The ultimate goals of mastering your schedule are to lower your stress level, increase you sense of accomplishment and maximize your effectiveness, while still keeping everybody reasonably happy and providing yourself with needed discretionary time. Take the time to learn and employ these techniques; I assure you, they'll make all the difference in your quality of life.*
> *Love,*
> *Dad*

## Chapter 15  Dealing With
## Personal Demons & Accepting Who
## You Are

"A man's true state of power and riches is to be in himself."  Henry Ward Beecher

*Dear Erin,*
*In order to reach your full potential and be truly*
*happy, you need to understand and come to terms*
*with your personal demons; the ultimate goal*
*being to accept yourself for who you are.  You*
*must be comfortable in your own skin.  This may,*
*or may not require a lot of self-assessment; it all*
*depends upon your personal state of affairs. . . .*

## SELF-ASSESSMENT

The first step to coming to terms with who you are is taking a long, hard look in the mirror, assessing your strengths and weaknesses. This will give you an idea of the basic tools with which you have to work.

I warn you, self-assessment can be upsetting. In fact, you may need to assess yourself in small doses, tackling one thing at a time. It can be very difficult because of all the different influences and factors that can get in the way. These 'road blocks' can help you develop your very own set of personal fears.

## FEAR

All of us accumulate a collection of fears that can infiltrate and negatively impact every aspect of our lives, **if we let them take control.**

The thing to remember about personal demons is that most, if not all, initially stem from fear of some kind. For the most part, they are:

**Fear of Rejection-** Whether we're criticized, dumped, neglected, or fired, rejection can be very difficult to deal with.

**Fear of Inadequacy-** That feeling many of us have when we don't feel good / smart / strong / attractive / quick / etc enough.

**Fear of Being Alone-** If you aren't comfortable with who you are or where you are in life, it can be tough being alone by yourself with all the time in the world to think about your discomfort.

**Fear of the Unknown-** No one is immune to this fear. We've all had moments when we feel lost and scared, not knowing what lies ahead.

Michael Pritchard, acclaimed keynote speaker, wellness coach and youth guidance motivator says this about fear, 'Fear is that little darkroom where negatives get developed.' Truer words were never spoken.

### PERSONAL DEMONS

Personal demons can develop from personal fears. They work to keep you in place, unable to move forward. Some people wind up in an endless cycle, repeating the same errors over and over again, incapable of thinking or acting in new and different patterns.

One way many people choose to deal with their personal demons is by not confronting them at all. Instead, they look for ways to avoid or hide from them. This is how many addictions start. It's often easier to numb yourself, than to do what's necessary to understand, work through and rid yourself of your fears.

### ADDICTION

Almost everyone has an addiction or addictions of some kind. Many are completely harmless and insignificant, such as me doing the L.A. Times crossword puzzle everyday online. Your mom's love of chocolate would be another. Harmless addictions aren't what I'm talking about. It's the debilitating ones that need to be looked at.

In today's world, by far the most crippling of addictions would be illegal drug use. While the 'drug du jour' will continually change as new and different ones promising even better highs become available, drug addiction can have utterly devastating effects.

When I was younger, it was felt that cocaine wasn't addictive; consequently its recreational use became widespread. Look how wrong that belief was! I know many people whose lives were completely destroyed by cocaine addiction.

Some people think that extreme drug use is the exception to the rule. They may even feel some drugs, like marijuana, are okay because their use doesn't necessarily lead to more serious drugs and/or dependency. That may all be true, but I assure you almost **all** drug addicts started out just smoking a little weed, thinking it wasn't a big deal. We all feel it couldn't happen to us. Well Erin, drug use is not something with which you can live because **addiction could happen to you.**

Smoking and drinking are two more damaging habits that affect great numbers of people today.

Smoking is, by far, one of the hardest habits to break. Nicotine is one of the most addictive drugs there is. When I was trying to quit smoking, my brain was its own worst enemy. I was used to feeling a certain way and my brain wanted to continue feeling that way-**no matter what**. It craved nicotine and I had to constantly pay attention to that craving so that I wouldn't give into it. It was several months before I could comfortably ignore any sudden urges. Decades later, I'm quite certain smoking just one cigarette or cigar would lead to my chain smoking all over again.

In my opinion, drinking is the most insidious addiction of all. It's the perfect dependency. With its social acceptability, availability and perceived positive affects in the short term (i.e. increased sociability, lessened inhibitions, etc.), it's very easy to fall into the trap of increased consumption. The use of alcohol is even promoted in many social circles as a way to better fit in with the crowd. Some people eventually figure out that alcohol's benefits are nothing more than smoke and mirrors and decrease their use of it on their own. Unfortunately though, many more head down the road of alcoholism.

Any detrimental addictions must be overcome and/or strictly controlled. If you can't rein them in, they'll compromise your health, hinder your career, destroy your personal relationships, bankrupt you and even leave you with serious legal problems. It just isn't worth exposing yourself to this kind of risk, Erin.

Before you ever get to the point where a dependency/addiction takes control of your life, please spend some time thinking about what you could be throwing away with that kind of self-destructive behavior. Get to the bottom of your issues and find a way to rid yourself of your personal demons (A.K.A. personal baggage).

### ADDRESS THE ISSUES

It doesn't matter how you choose to unload your personal baggage or what it may be. Whether you need to seek professional help, start writing in a personal journal, or confront the issues and/or people directly, get your negative influences out of the way so you feel better about yourself and can work on more positive endeavors.

Somewhere in this book, I mentioned how I had a very hard time coming to terms with my life when I turned thirty. For me, reaching this milestone was very traumatic -a mid-life crisis, if you will. I was totally dissatisfied with every aspect of my life.  One of the things I did during this time was talk to a professional.

I started seeing a psychologist in the hopes it would help me figure out what was going on inside.  Within a few sessions, we established I was suffering from moderately severe anguish causing me anxiety.  Although I wasn't suffering from panic attacks, I can tell you I felt poorly most of the time.

After seeing my counselor for 8 or 10 sessions, we had an ending meeting.  She literally told me there wasn't anything further with which she could help me.  I understood what the issues were and what I needed to do to resolve them.  So you see?  It was up to me to take the bull by the horns and right my own ship.

Dealing with my anxiety took a lot of soul searching.  I had to sort through all the negativity I was feeling and figure out what I really wanted for myself out of life.  If you ever find yourself feeling this way, don't try and run from it.  Take some time and make yourself think about whatever issues are weighing on you.  Until you can do this, they'll never really get settled so you can get closure.

A mindset I've adopted that has been a great help to me in dealing with whatever life throws my way is focusing on the present, not dwelling on the past.

I'm currently reading a biography about the life of Warren Buffett, someone I greatly admire.  He has an interesting way of looking at things, never dwelling on past unpleasant events, or cluttering his brain with what he considers useless drivel.  To him, his memory's like a bathtub.  He fills it with ideas, events and information that are of interest and, when he thinks this retained information is no longer germane, he pulls the plug, draining the tub. This allows room for new useful, pertinent and/or enjoyable subjects.

To some extent, I subscribe to Mr. Buffett's methodology. Utilizing this kind of thinking has enabled me to put aside otherwise onerous emotional baggage so I'm not dwelling on many of the bad experiences I've suffered through in my life. They're still a part of my personal library where I can reference them if necessary, but I'm able to keep my mind freed up to live life without these thoughts and memories constantly in my way.

Something else I've learned is it doesn't do you any good to drive yourself crazy by thinking about all the possible outcomes of any given situation. Idle speculation can needlessly raise your level of anxiety exponentially to no avail. You can sit there and work yourself up into a real dither by worrying about an outcome when, in all likelihood, the end result will be one on which you never counted. That isn't to say you should never speculate, but whenever you catch yourself in the act, immediately stop and take a deep breath. There are just too many things in life outside of your control. Work on and concern yourself with things you can influence.

### SUMMARY

If someone out there is using drugs or alcohol as an escape from their feelings, I suggest trying to face them just once. For one night, don't take anything. I bet you'll be in for a surprise. I bet you manage to get through it. And then, guess what? If you keep facing your fears they'll slowly diminish and end up in proper perspective. That's how I ultimately conquered mine. Facing them and making changes wherever I felt I needed to. You can't change your life in a day, but you can start heading in a new direction.

Experts spend a lot of time pontificating on what an addiction is and what you should do to break free from it. Ultimately it comes down to you. You have to come to the realization that you have a problem and accept responsibility for your actions. Blaming someone else for a problem does nothing to change your circumstances.

Erin, always remember that everyone makes mistakes-including you. On your journey through life there are bound to be countless bumps in the road and many wrong turns made. Don't be afraid to take a different turn or even turn around and start over again if necessary.

Even if you're mired in fear and self-doubt, unwilling to face anything or anybody, at the end of the day you'll be the one who makes the difference. You'll be the one who decides whether to pull yourself out of your dilemma or not. You'll be the one who decides drugs are not for you. You'll be the one who decides when enough is enough. You'll be the one who decides you want to end up in a better place.

One of the songs in my 'Dealing with Life' music list is "Drive" by the group Incubus. The theme of the song is never let the fear take the wheel and steer your way through life. You need to maintain control of where you're headed.

*. . . I've heard it said and it bears repeating here, that the difference between a champ and a chump is you! Promise me you won't ever let excuses, circumstances or other people get in your way of being you!*
*Love,*
*Dad*

# CHAPTER 16 SOME WAYS ATTITUDES CHANGE WITH AGE

"One's destination is never a place, but rather a new way of looking at things."     Henry Miller

*Dear Erin,*
*Through life experience and the realization of what's truly important and what isn't, your attitudes and viewpoints will change with age. Ideally you'll end up being a more patient and settled soul, more accepting of the ways of the world and a master of a simpler life. . . .*

Recently I had a conversation with my friend, Tim. Tim's my age and shares many of the same beliefs and opinions I do. Overall, he's a conservative thinking, moral and hard working individual whom I admire. We've had many off the cuff discussions in the past but this one, in particular, stands out for me.

It began with Tim asking a simple question, "Have you ever noticed how as you get older, you need fewer and fewer things"? I took all of two seconds to think about it and the answer was 'yes!' In fact, it's amazing at how little it really takes to make most people happy. The rest of the day, I thought about how I wish I'd come to this realization years before.

It prompted me to ask the same question of many other people I know and the response was almost unanimous: as we age, we tend to want to streamline and simplify; we're less willing to deal with clutter and nonsense, our overall attitude about life changes.

One great thing older folks tend to do (myself included) is stop and smell the roses. Simple things in life take on greater significance and meaning. Things that had long gone unnoticed begin to be appreciated. The pace at which one thinks, plans and acts most assuredly becomes more leisurely and enjoyable, less stressful and frenetic.

With age, while many elements of your personality remain intact, some of the hard edges soften as part of an overall mellowing process. Patience often increases and tempers tend to flare less frequently, with far less intensity. These types of changes are not only good for the person experiencing them, but also for the people with whom they come in contact.

Mellowing will play other roles as well. I notice that I worry less about how people perceive me than I did when I was younger. As a young man, I was constantly concerned about my image. These days, I still care about it, but I'm more comfortable in my own skin, so I'm less concerned with being judged.

Conversely, when I deal with people, whether I know and like them or not, I'm much more tolerant of them today than I would have been even 5 years ago. It's because I better understand and appreciate the idiosyncrasies we have that make us each unique.

As I've grown older, my concept of priorities has continually evolved. Over time, the list of important things has gotten shorter and its content has become less material-based and more emotionally/personally fulfilling.

Many times a change in attitude is brought about by a defining moment or moments in one's life; I've had my share. One of the first and by far the most impactful for me was when I was twenty-five and 'living large'.

When I was a young man, I was focused on chasing after the almighty dollar for whatever enjoyment it could buy me. Instant gratification was of paramount importance and I really didn't care who got hurt in the process. As I've told many of the friends I have today, you probably wouldn't have liked me very much back then.

It was during this time I inherited the nickname, "Fop". Look that up in your Funk & Wagnall! I spent money like it was water on wine, women, song and then some. I never saved a dime and lived well beyond my means. The image I projected to the outside world was critical to me. Looking good made me feel good. I was bullet proof and having the time of my life so.... Let the good times roll, right?

My outlook on life first started to change when I turned twenty-five. I'd been smoking for many, many years. I was considered a chain smoker, smoking at least two packs a day, but up to three or four depending on my mental state. I believed it somehow relaxed me, while at the same time made me look cool.

One day when I was showering I noticed I had a lump in my lower back. This worried me, so I went to the doctor who thought same day surgery should be scheduled immediately. He suspected it to be a cyst of some sort, but it was large enough to concern him.

Once on the operating table, under local anesthetic and cut open, he informed me it was a fatty tumor. I had two choices: to be closed up and re-scheduled for a more extensive procedure, or I could allow him to finish. I told him to proceed.

The nerve-wracking part of the surgery on my back was waiting several days afterwards until they analyzed the tumor to see if it was cancerous or not. Talk about rocking my world! This was the most traumatic ordeal I'd ever faced. I started thinking about the years I hadn't taken care of myself at all, smoking like a chimney and drinking like a fish. What would I do if I really did have cancer? I wasn't so bullet proof after all.

As I waited what seemed like forever for the test results, I quit smoking cold turkey (we didn't have pharmaceutical aids to help you stop smoking back then). I also began doing some soul searching: I started thinking about how badly I'd treated people in the past; how I hadn't spent enough time and/or cared about the people in my life that really cared about me; how I wished I'd taken better care of myself.

Lucky for me, this whole episode ended on a happy note. I didn't have cancer. What a relief! The outcome helped create the framework of the kinder and gentler Randy people know today. It stopped me from taking life for granted.

One piece of the attitude evolution that happens with aging is the realization of how much in life is beyond your control. You can try to exercise influence over many different things, but most of them are also affected by the actions of others and/or fate, areas well outside of your control. Erin, this is true for everyone, without exception, so I can only suggest that as you grow older, you learn to go with the ebb and flow.

Part of going with the flow is the realization that just because you're looking for certain things to happen, doesn't mean they will, or that they'll happen when you want them to. I never realized this when I was younger, but life's events and circumstances will happen in their own time, some would say, "in God's perfect time." Let me illustrate what I mean.

It's been three months since I was laid off from my job. While I have some prospects, there doesn't seem to be anything concrete on the immediate horizon. Your mom and I discussed one of my recent job prospects and the likelihood of whether it will pan out or not. As you can probably imagine, three months out of work has me feeling really cooped up and anxious. Your mom made a good point, 'He (the business owner) doesn't care that you're out of work. He only cares about what's best for his business, so he'll pull the trigger when he's ready to, not a moment sooner'. How right she is! This opportunity, if it happens, will happen in its own time frame, regardless of the fact that I may want him to hire me this instant.

Hopefully your life will reach a point where your personal state of affairs is in order. With less to worry about, you end up with more productive time available. For example, even though writing this book is a huge commitment for me, I now seem able to devote the time and effort needed for its completion. One reason is, having developed a patient and analytical approach to things. I'm more mentally prepared for the challenge. The other reason is all my ducks are in a row.

With time and experience most, if not all, aspects of life stabilize and are more easily brought under control. We've already talked about simplifying and eliminating clutter and nonsense. This will carry throughout all areas of day-to-day living. For example, you'll probably owe less money to fewer creditors. Cash or checks become more the norm, as opposed to charging purchases on credit. Purchases in general will be less frequent because you don't need or want as much. You get the idea.

> *. . . Erin, here's hoping as you age you'll find the*
> *results as satisfying as I have.*
> *Love,*
> *Dad*

## CHAPTER 17   K.I.S.S.

"Happiness consists of three things; Someone to love, work to do, and a clear conscience."   Author Unknown

*Dear Erin,*
*I've found one secret to a happier life is to **keep it** simple and stupid, hence the title for this chapter. Because we're extremely complex and emotional biochemical organisms with the abilities to think and reason, we have a tendency to make our lives complicated. A simpler life and lifestyle leaves a person more time to savor that which is important to them. . . .*

**RULES FOR A TRUE KISS LIFE:**

**1. Know Right from Wrong.** What a simple concept this is! Throughout our lives we're given endless examples of this fundamental belief, yet people persist in distorting what's truly right and somehow using it for personal gain. Erin, manipulating the truth is lying as an art; unacceptable. Know the difference between right and wrong and lead by example.

**2. Follow the Golden Rule, "Do unto others as you would have them do unto you."** The Golden Rule has a very long history and is the base from which social ideals, as well as human rights, have been established. It's used in determining what is and what is not just, ethical treatment of others; it's the standard by which countless conflicts have been resolved.

What The Golden Rule means for you is simple: Strive to give others the same level of respect and consideration you expect in return. Abiding by this principle will help to keep your dealings with others more positive and pleasant. It'll also help establish your reputation as a 'good guy'.

**3. Don't let someone else's karma become yours.** This is difficult, even though the words are self-explanatory. It's human nature to want revenge when something unjust or downright wrong befalls you. Usually, once you've had time to think things over rationally, you'll come to the conclusion that revenge is neither worth your time nor your effort; it's much more productive to devote your energy to more worthwhile pursuits. The Bible says, "Let he who is without sin, cast the first stone." I'm not a stone thrower. Take the high road and always treat others with decency in spite of how they may treat you.

**4. Don't go back on your word.** Look at this! Here's another of the K.I.S.S. rules that can be pretty challenging to follow. Always keep your promises. Always honor your vows. Your word is your bond.

**5. Take pride in your work.** In today's world look at how many things are done in a sub-standard way! Products are made with increasingly poorer quality, planned obsolescence being the goal. Workers try to stretch out their jobs so they can bleed employers for every possible dime. Individuals shirk responsibility and pass the buck. People do half-assed jobs maintaining and running their households, automobiles and finances. Whatever you do should be done well enough that you'd have no problem signing your name to it.

If you find yourself in any situation where you aren't allowed to operate under that premise, get out. Go someplace where you won't have to compromise yourself or your principals. You always want to be proud of what you leave in your wake.

**6. Finish what you start.** This is important for maintaining your sanity, as well as establishing your dependability.

If I have fifty unfinished tasks staring me in the face, my stress level escalates and adversely affects everything and everybody else around me. I'd much rather have some completed tasks, with those not yet begun, prioritized. Finish one thing before going on to the next. Maintain your focus.

**7. Don't ever ignore common sense.** When you aren't sure how to proceed in any given situation, rely on your common sense. It amazes me how many people forget they possess the ability to reason and rationalize in order to come up with a sensible conclusion/decision.

Now that I've given you a list of my rules for 'KISS living', I'm going to explain ways in which I simplify my day-to-day life.

I generally try to keep my life as uncluttered and pleasant as possible in order to keep my stress level to a minimum. I try to limit my exposure to some of what I perceive as the uglier aspects of life.

One of my personal bugaboos is dealing with daily mail. I can't stand it! Ninety percent of the mail we get these days is junk. The balance is monthly bills. In order to limit my exposure to this source of my personal stress, I have a post office box. I check it once a week and your mom checks it once a week. Guess what? The world doesn't come to an end because we don't pick up my mail every day. All the bills still get paid and everyone's happy.

E-mail can be a source of stress for me too. I try to keep away from it as much as possible when I'm home. I have to check it during the weekend for work-related issues, but I keep that to a minimum. There's no point in causing myself undue stress when I'm most likely not in any kind of position to address many of the issues contained therein.

Communication technology overload is something from which most of us suffer today. What began as e-mail and cell phones, progressed to include instant messaging, Facebook, blogs and Twitter. There's no end in sight, but people like me are starting to tune out and turn off.

Erin, here's something I recommend: Shut your cell phone off for select periods so you can have 'quiet time'. I know it works for me. Even if it's only for a short while, it may make all the difference in your mental state.

Get rid of useless clutter. Whether you have a garage sale, donate old books to the library, or have a dumpster brought in, make it go away. I'll never forget when we lived in New Milford I had a ten yard dumpster delivered. I felt we had lots of useless crap we should make go away.

I'm sure some people thought we'd never fill it. In the end, we filled that dumpster and then some.

Always try to travel as light as possible. For example, I work with many people who feel the need to carry several bags with them back and forth between work and home. Over and over again, everyday they haul a load of crap with them. Some alternatives would be to send e-mails to yourself that you can reference, or to carry a flash drive on which files can be loaded. You'll feel better not lugging stuff around with you all the time.

If at all possible, leave work at work. I know in today's world the line is blurred between professional and personal time, but try to set up limits as to how much work you'll allow in your home and vice versa. If you work at home one or two days a week, don't spend any additional time working at home on top of that. Oh, and when you have time off (vacation, holiday, etc.), don't call into work. When you're away, be away!

Something else to remember is not to overload your social calendar. There are times where my presence is requested and I just have to say 'no'. Maybe work has been extra stressful, or I feel I've already been out gallivanting too much. Whatever the reason, I know I wouldn't be good company because I just don't want to attend! Don't be afraid to tell your friends and family that you can't make it if you aren't up to it.

The same holds true for charity and/or volunteer efforts in which friends may try to get you involved. You need to be in a 'good place' with your life before you can devote your time to these endeavors. You're better off not getting directly involved if it would spread you too thin. One way I've worked around being actively involved in charity efforts is by explaining that I don't have the time to devote (I legitimately don't right now) and asking if I could make a donation instead.

> *. . . Erin, the purpose of living a 'KISS life' is to maximize and enjoy as much of life as possible. You need not always run at 100 miles an hour in an effort to accomplish everything that others think you should. I want you to be able to stop and smell the roses if you choose. Remember, it's your life Erin - KISS.*
> *Love,*
> *Dad*

# CHAPTER 18 THE POWER OF POSITIVE THINKING

"Events will take their course; it is no good of being angry at them. He is happiest who wisely turns them to the best account." Euripides

*Dear Erin,*

*Let's talk about the importance of developing a positive attitude.*

*The power of positive thinking can be life changing. Its presence or absence can color your perception of everything around you. Your thoughts can influence all aspects of your physical, emotional and mental wellbeing. Learning how to use them to your advantage will help enrich your life.*

*. . .*

The very first thing you need to understand is that happiness is a state of mind requiring continual work, sometimes very hard work, to achieve and maintain. One reason so many people choose to be unhappy is because it takes no effort at all. All you need do is listen to all the negativity in your midst. It can be very easy to get caught up in it and join in the chorus of 'poor me'. So Erin, it's imperative you make a conscious decision as to how you'll look at things each and every day. Is your glass half empty or half full?

Let me tell you about a friend of mine, Curtis. Curtis is a middle-aged, divorced, father of two with a decent job in a large corporation. He's likeable and has many strong friendships (like his and mine) that have endured for decades. Curtis is very self-reliant, responsible and intelligent. He's also somewhat cynical in his view of the world, with a touch of bitterness thrown in for good measure. Curtis is quite an interesting personality to be sure. In years past, I, along with many others, have sought his advice and counsel.

I stopped seeking his counsel after listening to him pontificate one evening. The one quote of his that has remained with me all these years was: "Life is simply a chain of events and/or things you can't have". Wow!! Think about that. What an awful way to feel about your life! Curtis' quote and attitude spoke volumes to me about him and reminded me that I never want to share his view.

By the way, many people hold a similar view. Erin, the first thing you need to remember in developing and maintaining a positive mental attitude: Don't walk away from negative people - **Run**!

In your quest of improving your general outlook on life, it's important to work on building up your mental defenses to help guard against any negative influences trying to infiltrate your thought processes. You can't let your guard down for a minute. This includes the times when your own thoughts will attempt to conspire against you. Let me give you an example of what I mean.

During my recent lay-off, I was at home writing one afternoon when a random negative thought rushed into my head: 'I feel like a cigarette butt. Like I've been passed around for everyone to take a drag from and the last guy just snuffed me out'. No comment on how weird this thought was, please.

If I hadn't consciously taken control of my brain at that moment, that idiotic notion would've taken root, leaving me sad or depressed. Instead, I decided to look at the positives of my unemployment situation. One of the things I started focusing on was how this was a golden opportunity for me to begin a whole new challenging career path.

Once I started thinking positively, within minutes I felt much better and more confident. After a short time, the cigarette butt thought was completely gone, without a trace. I was again feeling like a worthwhile person with a meaningful existence. The only reason I even remember it, is because I wrote it down the moment it happened.

Sometimes your brain will start analyzing different situations and offer up various solutions from which to choose. Some will be completely outlandish while others may have merit. Then, of course, there will be negatively slanted options. Try to sort through them all and objectively select one that will leave you in a more positive position then before. Again, let me offer up an example.

This morning I was reviewing some notes my editor had e-mailed me concerning this chapter. One option she mentioned was if I don't end up with enough useful information in this chapter for it to stand alone, we could add it in with material elsewhere. At first blush, it sounds like a reasonable solution doesn't it? But look a little deeper. I didn't like this option because I want to fix this chapter. How could I possibly allow myself to fail when writing a chapter about positive thinking? That would be negative and I'm not a negative person. So, I've decided to enlist my editor's help instead of simply throwing in the towel. Failure is just not an option!

Your thought processes can spawn self-fulfilling prophecies, Erin. I'm sure you've heard of them. A self-fulfilling prophecy is where a thought you have becomes so intense and overpowering, you start to believe in it. You may even modify your behavior sub-consciously in an effort to reinforce the thought further. For all intents and purposes, you end up influencing the possible outcomes of your life through this behavior.

Usually when people refer to self-fulfilling prophecies, they think of them in a negative context. Why not, instead, create them so they'll work in your favor? If you can learn to harness the power of positive thought and then use it to create self-fulfilling prophecies, great things can happen. Okay, how do you begin thinking along these lines?

Seeing things in a positive light can be very difficult for some people. It may be easier to start out small, assessing one situation or circumstance at a time. Take a step back from a particular issue and look at it objectively. Is it really significant? Does it really matter? Most importantly, "Is this issue something with which I should be concerned?" You'd be amazed how much time and energy can be wasted pondering things that don't really matter or that shouldn't concern **you**. Work at getting to the point where you can eliminate the nonsense and concentrate on what's essential.

Sometimes, what makes it difficult to maintain a positive mental attitude is your own bio-chemical make-up. There are so many internal influences and conditions affecting your general wellbeing; consistency, at times, can be elusive.

For example, today I was in a terrible funk. It took a good deal of my concentration to avoid depression. I think the weather had a lot to do with it. It was a very raw and dreary day out, the kind of day where you just want to crawl under a blanket and go back to sleep. I managed to take a nap, allowing me to regain some of my focus and start writing!

Here's a simple way to get out of a funk and back on track: When you wake up in the morning, tell yourself you're going to forget about what happened yesterday. You're going to start the new day with a clean slate. Picture yourself rebooting your computer. Hit the "Ctrl, Alt and Delete" keys. You can even post a couple sticky notes as reminders on your bathroom mirror and by the coffeemaker - "Ctrl Alt Delete ☺". Perhaps you prefer this reminder – "Will the glass be half-empty or half-full today? I CHOOSE HALF FULL!"

They say in order to create a new habit pattern, you need to do something consistently, the same way, for thirty days. Whether it's 30, 60 or 90 don't take the sticky notes down until your positive, 'good morning attitude' becomes automatic. I promise you it will.

Here's another trick I use that may work for you: I'll often address an issue I'm having right before falling asleep. It usually isn't anything too major, but often something that's troubling me. Let's say, for example I've been having a hard time sleeping and it's really been bringing me down mentally. Right before I fall asleep, I'll draft a simple statement in my mind; something like: 'Tomorrow when I wake up, I'll feel completely refreshed'. Instead of counting sheep, I'll repeat this phrase over and over again in my mind, until I drop off to sleep. Guess what? Every time I've ever done it, I end up feeling great the next morning. Even when I've had next to no sleep after a late night, I still wake up feeling like a new man.

You should be able to use this technique to help address other issues as well. The only thing I'd suggest is that you encapsulate whatever it is in a brief statement that's easy to repeat and remember. I believe this kind of mental repetition to be a type of self-hypnosis, although I'm not an expert in that field and I'm not considered to be a somnambulistic person.

Sometimes the hard work involved in being positive and happy may require a full-blown propaganda campaign. You've heard the phrase used 'putting the right spin on it'? There will be times you may need to be a politician with yourself, cheering yourself on as if you were attending a pep rally so you can get back on the right track.

If you ever find yourself stuck in a negative state of mind, it can be difficult to see much beyond day-to-day, or week-to-week. You end up simply taking care of your most pressing needs and not much else. This is one of the ways people can end up in a rut. Life isn't very pleasant when you're watching it pass you by while you're stuck in a rut. You need to do whatever's necessary to snap out of it. Remember in the movie 'Moonstruck' when Loretta's mom tells her: 'Loretta your life's going down the toilet'. Don't allow that to happen to you.

If you find you're in the midst of life's trials and tribulations, keep busy doing productive, constructive things. Forward progression by accomplishing even the smallest of things can help keep you from slipping into a funk. Erin, there's another old saying (I know I have a million of them, but remember I've been around awhile): 'An idle mind is the devil's workshop'. Well, it's true. You can really start to beat yourself up if your thoughts get away from you. Keeping busy with purposeful endeavors can prevent that from happening.

Can I guarantee that using these techniques will work 100% of the time? Of course not! You live with me; you see that I have my moments just as everyone does. But you also see how quickly I recover from them. That's because when I'm having difficulties trying to maintain my positive outlook on life, I think about everything I'm writing here and then work on adjusting my attitude. Practice makes perfect.

. . . *Remember Erin, the glass can be half full or half empty; it's all up to you. You can decide whether you want to focus on excuses for failure, or reasons to succeed and be happy. You can choose to look at things from the standpoint of personal needs and wants (a negative point of view-the glass half empty), or to look at them from the standpoint of being satisfied with what you have (a much more positive point of view-the glass half full). Make the right choice!*

*Love,*

*Dad*

## CHAPTER 19  AGE IS A NUMBER & OLD IS AN ATTITUDE

"It is a mistake to regard age as a downhill grade towards dissolution.  The reverse is true.  As one grows older, one climbs with surprising strides."
George Sand

*Dear Erin,*
*I want to discuss growing old and aging.  It probably isn't a subject you've thought much about yet.  When you're an up and coming, gorgeous, young woman, why would you?  Your whole life is still ahead.  Growing old isn't even on your radar.  Sooner or later, though, you'll have to deal with the reality that old age will happen to you; you won't live forever.  Let's see if I can help prepare you for some of what lies ahead. . . .*

I'm constantly amazed at the spectrum of effects the aging process has on different people; each ends up with their own unique set of issues. Some seem to age at an accelerated rate while others seem 'timeless', not aging at all.

I consider myself very lucky. Many people mistake me for someone at least ten years younger than I am. My mom, your Grandma Nancy, has always looked young for her age. Her mother was Norwegian; her father, Navajo. She is one of the most attractive women you'll ever set eyes on. I'm blessed to have inherited some of those special genes.

I don't have much gray hair (in fact I don't have much hair at all) or many wrinkles; neither did my maternal grandparents. Those details aside, the overriding difference between me and many other 55-year olds is my attitude. In many respects, I just 'think younger'.

Recently, I found myself in the middle of an interesting three-way conversation between your mom, her cousin David's wife, Cindy, and me. We were all attending the wedding of your mom's cousin, John. Throughout our discourse, Cindy kept interjecting how old the event made her feel. This happened repeatedly until I felt the need to speak up.

It's important you fully understand who the people in this discussion were. Both your mom and Cindy are attractive, successful, energetic, forty-something moms. I don't understand why either one of them should be concerned with age and/or mortality. I chimed in to say that I hoped they were kidding; neither of them was old, by a long shot, as far as I was concerned!

My comments were dismissed with 'It's different for men'. I persisted, saying neither one of them had anything to worry about. The conversation ended on a statement made by your mom, supported by Wendy: "The reason for the male vs. female difference in attitude with respect to aging is because men can continue reproducing, if they so desire." I don't agree with that hypothesis, but it was definitely the end of the conversation. I knew if I tried to continue the discussion, it would fall on deaf ears.

Later that evening, I brought up the discussion again with your mom. After some prodding, she attempted to substantiate her position by saying older men are perceived differently than older women. They're seen as becoming more powerful with age, while a woman is seen as being used up. And older men often desire younger women.

This whole conversation brings up a valid point about aging: If you're uncomfortable with the physical changes that are likely to occur, then you'll have difficulty adjusting to the aging process, regardless of your gender.

These physical changes can have a profound effect on one's perceived sexuality. Women are the most influenced by them. It can be difficult adapting to the evolution of your appearance that age brings with it - the fear being you'll end up somehow less desirable.

Some people lash out at the changes age brings. Many go through a mid-life crisis at some point, temporarily unable to cope. These episodes can last for an indeterminate length of time before you begin to realize how ridiculous they are. No one can outrun old age.

Many women express that their children leaving the nest and going off on their own is one of the biggest challenges they face in their aging process. This challenge tends to be coupled with concerns for finding a new purpose, once mothering has been put on the back burner. Some people would argue this to be a huge difference for women versus men. As I watch you growing up, preparing to make your way through life, I'm not so sure we men aren't susceptible to some similar feelings.

While I can't say how you'll change as you age, I can strongly suggest you try to go with the flow. You can't change the inevitable; spend your time and energy working on things you can influence. Erin, the primary rule for dealing with growing old is: Always do the best you can with what you have. Look at your Grandpa!

I talk with Grandpa every Sunday morning. As you know, at this stage of his life he's mostly confined to his wheelchair. He suffers from gradually declining health, but he doesn't ever complain. He just gets on with it every single day and does his best to take care of Grandma Tammy's and his needs. I ask him every week how he's doing and how life in Delaware's going. His response is almost always the same. 'I'm doing okay as long as you don't ask for the details'. He's a good example of always doing the best you can with what you have. You could learn a lot from him.

There's a saying, "You're as young as you feel." Do you want to feel young? Try thinking in terms of what projects you **can** tackle and what challenges you **can** conquer. There are two kinds of people: Those who will tell you they can't do it; and those who will tell you **how** they did it.

Don't waste a minute thinking about all the things you can't do; focus your attention on putting your remaining resources to good use.

I have very little patience with people whose only goal left in life is to fill up their social calendars with wall-to-wall doctors' appointments. Their only conversation topics tend to be endless speculation of their possible new 'malady du jour.' And some doctors play right along, thinking if they find some new and exotic illness, they're doing these patients favors. Utterly ridiculous to me!

Many times, these very 'woe-is-me' folks live alone and have inadequate social interaction, whether it's activity or just plain conversation with others. Their health and mortality become their single focus because, guess what? They've shut themselves off from everything else. It's more common among the elderly than you'd think and it's a habit that develops slowly over a period of time. They sink into it gradually, like a warm bath, and it becomes familiar and comfortable to them. Therefore, one of the things you need to avoid as you age is isolating yourself from the world around you. Persist in putting forth the necessary effort to 'engage', so you don't disengage and disappear.

There are people in the world, younger than me, who've already started feeling and acting 'old'. Needless to say, I don't spend much time around them. First of all, I can't identify with the mindset. Secondly, remember what I've said about staying away from negative people.

To me, it's such a shame to throw in the towel and start limiting yourself just because you've reached middle age. In my mind, 'middle-aged' means there's a lot of time remaining and many things to accomplish.

I have plenty of days where I feel lousy, but I don't dwell on it. It's no big deal to me that I'm no longer 20 or 30 years old. Today, I have a much better sense of what I can achieve mentally and physically without 'jamming on the gas pedal' as hard as I used to. I've found it much better to do most things in moderation. Slower and steadier often wins the race.

Something else I've never understood is how a person could let their life be completely dictated by others. For example, some parents are so devoted to their kids, they can't imagine life without them. In fact, many of these parents have absolutely no life of their own! Well, guess what? Somewhere along the way, kids leave home and start to live their own lives. Where does that leave those parents? It's a very painful reality that often slaps them squarely in the face. Erin, please don't ever neglect your life for the sake of other people, or things. After all it's YOUR life, no one else's!

You'll find a big part of aging gracefully is giving and receiving love. The love of family and friends is, by far, the most treasured possession any of us have. Some realize it sooner than others; their lives are all the more fulfilling for it.

There are people out there who hate the idea of growing old and spend all their time thinking about and longing for 'the good old days'. They wish they could turn back the clock and be 'young' again. This is a complete mystery to me! Why would anyone want to go back in time? Why suffer, once more, through all the mistakes made along the way? No thanks!

I've found a lot of good things about growing older. I'm much more analytical than when I was younger. I'm able to think and concentrate as never before, partly because I'm so much more patient. My finely aged reasoning skills have made me a much better problem solver.

I'm also able to tackle much larger projects than ever before; for example, writing this book. At this point in time, it's easier for me not to become overwhelmed by the enormity of the task. I can break it down into ideas, chapters and paragraphs. I now have a sound plan of attack for what would once have seemed an insurmountable challenge.

Erin, here's a biggie for you: At this stage of my life, I'm more empathetic and forgiving than I've ever been. Life has taught me to see things from other people's perspectives and understand them more fully.

Overall, with age and experience, you learn to care more. Not that you don't care for others now. I know you do! But as you age, you'll end up becoming more caring and giving. It's all part of a mellowing process that happens to the vast majority, at some point.

The mellowing process also affects your temperament. When I was younger, I was extremely volatile and unforgiving. It took very little to set off my temper, and boy did I hold grudges! Well, those days seem to be well behind me. Now it takes more to make me angry and my anger dissipates in a matter of minutes, sometimes seconds. When I say 'it's over', it really is. I no longer hold grudges and my life is better because of it!

I hope reading this, whether it's now or when you're a little older, will help you realize age is just a number.

What do I tell you guys every year at my birthday? It really isn't a big event for me. I don't ever look for special treatment beyond when we go out for dinner as a family. All another birthday means to me is I've completed another orbit. Don't get hung up on it whether you're turning 25 or 95. I like how Larry the Cable Guy responds when asked what year his birthday is: 'It's every year!'

> *. . . Erin, there's a baseball player named Chili*
> *Davis who's credited with saying: 'Growing old*
> *is mandatory; growing up is optional'. Almost*
> *every single happy older person I've ever met still*
> *has a touch of child in them. You can see the*
> *glint in their eyes, or their mischievous smile.*
> *Maybe they still have a spring in their step, or a*
> *great sense of humor. Erin, my hope for you is*
> *that you live a long and happy life and that you*
> *hold on to your inner child for as long as you can.*
> *Love,*
> *Dad*

## CHAPTER 20    RELIGION & SPIRITUALITY

"This is my simple religion. There is no need for temples; no need for complicated philosophy. Our own brain, our own heart is our temple; the philosophy is kindness." Dalai Lama

*Dear Erin,*
*As you make your way through life, your personal development will include some amount of soul searching, also known as seeking self-enlightenment. As you grow older, there's a natural curiosity that arises from within you to discover and understand what life's all about. You'll want to be more in tune with your authentic self. This journey invariably will include learning more about religion and/or spirituality. . .*

In my opinion, religion and spirituality are two of the most complex subjects to intelligently discuss and fully comprehend. I'd like to give it the old college try here because I think they're very important. Let's begin by defining them so we're on the same page.

**Religion** - belief in and reverence for a supernatural power or powers, regarded as creator and governor of the universe.

**Spirituality** - matters pertaining to the inner spirit; based on the idea that there exists something, whether it's a state of mind, a being, or a destination, that's outside the experience of our five human senses; the personal relationship of you as an individual to this state of mind and sacred ideas.

In addition, from Wikipedia, (one of my favorite websites to find out information on virtually any topic): Spirituality can refer to an ultimate reality or transcendent dimension of the world; an inner path enabling a person to discover the essence of his or her being, or the deepest values and meanings by which people live. Spiritual practices, including meditation, prayer and contemplation, are intended to develop an individual's inner life; bringing about a more comprehensive self.

While religion, spirituality and even morality are very closely related, they're by no means one and the same thing. Being truly religious can guide someone towards leading a spiritual and/or moral life, but living a moral and/or spiritual life doesn't necessarily mean you're religious.

Many different religious beliefs are touted as being the 'right one'. In fact, some people become belligerent and close-minded at the mere mention of any alternatives to their choice. What's most important is that you keep an open mind, develop your own set of beliefs and abide by them. As I like to say: Be your own person!

Some people looking for inspiration, me included, may journey to one of earth's mystical places: Machu Picchu in Peru, Glastonbury, England or one of my favorite places – Sedona, Arizona. While I can't vouch for the other places I mention, I can tell you when I was in Sedona, I felt as if everything was right with me and the world. I felt like I belonged there. I didn't want to leave – it was so calming for me being there.

Some people choose to devote their entire lives in the search for true spiritual enlightenment. A good example would be the Dalai Lama whose quote I used at the start of this chapter. There's a lot that can be learned from studying the teachings of different and diverse religious and spiritual tenets. Don't be afraid to explore them.

I'm a firm believer that the various religions of the world are nothing more than many paths to the same truth. Because I align myself to this way of thinking, I have no issue with whatever religion anyone chooses to observe, including you. It's purely a matter of individual choice and no one else's business to criticize or condemn. I hope you'll follow my lead in this regard. There's already more than enough bigotry, partisanship and ignorance in the world without trying to dictate to others how and what they should believe. And if someone truly does believe in a certain religion and/or path of spiritual teaching, you'll be wasting your breath trying to convince them otherwise.

Some people may believe in a Supreme Being, albeit not necessarily God, as you or I think of Him. The image you may have in your mind may be completely different than the one I have in mine or the one your best friend has. It makes no difference. We're all on the same page.

Something I strongly disagree with is how some followers of religion feel the need to proselytize. This practice violates one of my no-no's, 'Attempting to compel others to believe and live as we do'. When I'm curious about someone's religion, I'll ask about it. I'd much rather see more people genuinely 'walking the walk' and fewer simply "talking the talk".

Throughout your life, you'll meet plenty of people who go to church faithfully every Sunday and then lie, cheat and steal the rest of the week. That's nothing more than hypocrisy and not the way I want you to live your life. Erin, the lesson here is simple: If you choose to live according to the tenets of a religion, you need to do so whether it's convenient or not. It's a full-time, life long commitment.

It's important that you fully understand the choices you make and how they can affect the rest of your life. While having religious beliefs can help a person become more grounded and allow them to feel more fulfilled, they should never be used as a crutch. Your individual shortcomings should never be blamed on them. If the path you've selected for yourself puts you in a position where it can be detrimental to your individual development or even harmful to your physical wellbeing, you need to continue your search.  Your 'right path' should only ever help you to lead a more satisfying and fulfilling life.

On occasion, you may meet people who claim to be atheistic or agnostic.  They are, by far, the most difficult for me to deal with as I don't ascribe to those ways of thinking.  I've also found atheistic and agnostic people, in general, to be the most negative, therefore the most toxic.  I tend to avoid spending time in their company and I'd highly recommend you do the same.

Many people ultimately develop their own spiritual doctrine, often a blend of different religious and spiritual beliefs.  Some don't belong to an organized religion, but instead concentrate on living a good, clean, wholesome life and leaving a small footprint in their wake.  Buddhism refers to this as karmic law.  I'm sure you've heard of good and bad karma.

In the Bible, Galatians 6: 7-9 says, "Be not deceived; God is not mocked: for whatsoever a man soweth, that shall he also reap.  For he that soweth to his flesh shall of the flesh reap corruption; but he that soweth to the Spirit shall of the Spirit reap life everlasting.  And let us not be weary in well doing: for in due season we shall reap, if we faint not."  Living a wholesome life means the same thing in any language.

Part of living a good, clean, wholesome life is honestly caring about others and the world around you.  I'm not saying you literally have to love thy neighbor, but I hope you develop compassion for others as part of your spiritual development.  Erin, life's all about give and take; the emphasis placed on giving.

Some people will neglect their individual development and enlightenment in the pursuit of more selfish endeavors. Throughout this book I speak about many issues like being too career driven, too materialistic, too egocentric, etc. etc. None of these should ever get in the way of your spiritual development.

I'm sure you've heard about people that end up having regrets about where they ended up in their lives. Well, it often stems from ignoring your inner self. If you take nothing else from reading this - remember to spend time learning about you.

People often need a catalyst to help them think about whom they really are and how they want to lead their lives. I think my catalyst was when I met your mom. She opened my world up to more possibilities and the meaning of true love and forgiveness.

> *. . . Erin, I don't know what the catalyst will be*
> *that enables you to find your true self and*
> *discover your personal spiritual path. Maybe*
> *it'll be in reading this. But understanding the*
> *power of love and forgiveness is a prerequisite*
> *for living spiritually. The sooner you do, the*
> *sooner you can head out on your journey.*
> *Here's hoping you've already started!*
> *Love,*
> *Dad*

# CHAPTER 21 THOUGHTS ON MORTALITY AND DEATH

"Life can only be understood backwards, but it must be lived forward."    Soren Kierkegaard

*Dear Erin,*

*I want to impart some thoughts, ideas and observations for you to consider concerning mortality and death. While I believe certain decisions we make along the way can add or subtract from our time here, it's still limited. Don't waste any of it. Make the most of your life!*

I recently watched a movie called 'The Bucket List' starring Jack Nicholson and Morgan Freeman. It's a very touching story about two terminally ill men who meet while sharing a hospital room. Jack Nicholson's character is a millionaire who has led an extremely shallow, loveless life while Morgan Freeman is a poor man who seems to have had a life rich in love and family. They decide to live out their days together, experiencing all the things they've each missed out on in their respective lives. They compile a list of things they want to do before they die and go about doing them.

I don't want to get into the characters or theme too much, other than to say I consider it to be a 'must see' movie. It delivers a very important message: Don't go through life saying I should have, would have or could have. Get out and live so you're not left with any regrets.

Let me tell you about one of my heroes who lives her life in exactly this manner. Erin, as you know I recently started my new job in Massachusetts. It's a great distance from home; I needed to find a place to stay three nights a week and my Aunt Shirley has graciously opened up her home to me.

Five years ago, Aunt Shirley was facing the very real possibility of death from cancer. In May of 2005, she was given a clean bill of health from her doctor. In July of the same year, she was diagnosed with stage 4 ovarian cancer. The way this cancer was discovered was when one of the blood clots (caused by the cancer) let loose in her leg and traveled through her body. The clot went completely through her heart and exited at the other side.

After surviving her near death experience from the blood clot traveling through her heart and despite being given a grim prognosis, she never gave up, enduring whatever treatments the doctors prescribed. Today she's a happy, healthy and very active 75-year old woman who (and I quote), 'has a lot of living to do'.

Aunt Shirley spends a great deal of time loving and being loved by her family (including yours truly). She's very involved in the church and her local community and also has a great boyfriend and a very active social life. Always on the go, you'd never think of her as a senior citizen. Her goal is simply to enjoy her life to the fullest extent possible and, along the way, help others enjoy theirs. I wish everybody could spend time with her. She's an inspiration and the real deal.

Much like Aunt Shirley, I don't believe the thought or threat of death should ever be used as an excuse to give up living. Additionally, it should never be used as a way out. This means that suicide isn't something I would consider. In almost any situation you'll ever find yourself in, there's a better solution then simply giving up and throwing in the towel. Now that I've said that, there are exceptions to every rule.

While I don't personally believe that committing suicide is an acceptable alternative to facing life head on, I do believe there may be certain special circumstances where you earn the right to do whatever you deem appropriate for yourself.

I recently had a discussion with Grandpa about people being selfish with their lives. He feels that everyone should want to live as long as they can, no matter what.

Where does that leave people at the end of their lives who are in unimaginable pain, or so many others for whom an assisted suicide (by physician or loved one) may be the compassionate alternative?

Your Aunt brought up a good point: Isn't it a bit self-righteous to think that our way is the only way? Grandpa has said he wants to be kept alive at any cost, for as long as possible. Could it be he's just uncomfortable with anyone articulating an alternate plan for their end of life?

My hope for everyone is that they be allowed to choose for themselves. If they should decide to tough it out and continue fighting so they can remain here with us, great! But if not, who are we to argue? It's selfish to keep our loved ones here for our own comfort. Erin, is it our right to keep anyone in dire circumstances here against their wishes?

At this stage of my life, what worries me most about death is not the act of dying itself. I know, I'm a big, bad middle-aged guy who still thinks I have many years ahead of me. Maybe my attitude would be different if I suddenly had to face the reality of death. For now, I'm most worried about what I'll leave in my wake, when my time comes. For example, I don't want to leave you and your mom in some kind of hopeless financial situation. Your mom and I have had several discussions about this, yet this concern still looms large in my mind.

I'd like to leave behind something for you to remember me by, a legacy if you will. Maybe this book will be a part of it, who knows? I think everybody should strive to leave something more in this world than what they took.

Something else that's becoming more important to me as I grow older is in not leaving a lot of loose ends: a bunch of unfinished projects, unpaid bills or unfulfilled goals. The tidier things are, the happier I'll be when the time comes for me to go.

For many people, the thought of death can be overwhelming. Dwelling on it can strike terror in their hearts. If you can reach the point in your life where you're content with your place and what you've accomplished, I believe your fear of dying will diminish or even disappear all together. If you aren't yet at this plateau, my advice to you is to sit down and really look at what's important for you and how you can get there. Working towards a goal tends to be more gratifying than focusing on death and dying.

I don't spend a lot of time thinking about death. Some would say that's because I'm too afraid; I disagree. Why spend a lot of time thinking about something that will inevitably happen? Quite honestly, I'm too busy thinking of all the things I have yet to do.

If, when I'm gone, you smile whenever you think of me, then I'll feel like it's all been worthwhile. I hope you'll be proud of what I stood for, taught you and accomplished in my life. I hope your mom will think I was a good husband and that you'll think I was a great dad. This is the kind of stuff that's important, Erin.

Something worthy of your consideration is how you want to be celebrated when you do die. What kind of memorial do you want to have? What kind of service? How do you wish to be remembered?

*. . . Erin, when someone thinks of you, what kind of image do you want to bring to their mind? What is most memorable about you? If you've lived your life as completely and honestly as possible, the answers to these questions should be to your liking.*
*Love,*
*Dad*

# CHAPTER 22    DRINKING YOUR OWN KOOL-AID

"It is our choices, Harry, that show what we really
are, far more than our abilities."
Albus Dumbledore (Harry Potter)

*Dear Erin,*
*In the beginning of this book, I list the 'Six Mis-*
*takes of Man'. One of them is 'Attempting to com-*
*pel others to believe and live as we do'. My*
*intention in writing this book isn't to do that. It's*
*merely to offer you some 'time-tested' ideas and*
*food for thought. More importantly, this advice*
*comes from your dear old dad who loves you very*
*much and wants only the best for you. Erin, I'm*
*quite certain that following my advice will only*
*prove to enhance your life. . . .*

Now that I've brought you along for this ride through the last 21 Chapters about my outlook on life, it's time for you to start living your own. I hope you don't just read this book and put it up on a shelf in your library when you're finished. I believe its contents to be worthwhile; you would do well if the principles I've laid out became second nature to you. That having been said, let's look at what I call, "Drinking your own Kool-Aid."

Throughout your life, there will be occasions when you become disgusted with yourself and/or the circumstances in which you end up. Often when you feel this way, it's a result of your own doing. You may find yourself asking, "How did I get here? How did this happen?" Well, most likely it will have been the end result of a series of bad decisions made based on poor judgment. This is one example of what I call, "Drinking your own Kool-Aid." However, in these instances, you won't like the flavor very much at all.

Being human and therefore a creature of habit, it's easy to wind up facing similar circumstances, over and over again. You'll find it frustrating and that particular Kool-Aid will never taste any better. So what do you do?

When you want to change your results, you have to change the variables. In this case, it would involve getting back to the basics of using positive thinking and looking for new ideas or ingredients; "It's time to tweak the mix of Kool-Aid."

I just attended a two-day investment seminar where a positive mental attitude was stressed as being essential for your individual success. The speaker spelled out, very succinctly, the differences between the mindsets of poor, middle-class and rich people.

Before starting out on a new and different path, the type of person you want to be will dictate how you proceed and, often, where you end up.

For example:

A poor person will ask 'What if it doesn't work?'

A middle-class person will say 'I sure hope this works.'

A rich person will announce 'It'll work because I'm going to make it work.'

Rich people **expect** success. They realize they can't sit back and **wait** to be lucky, so they decide they're going to create opportunities for themselves - even where none existed before! Additionally, they have undying faith in their abilities, allowing no one and nothing to deter them.

Erin, that's what I want for you. I want you to choose the mindset or mantra you decide to live by, and then start to build your life accordingly and live it out loud. Choose the walk you want and walk it. Live, eat and breathe it. Drink your own Kool-Aid and enjoy the taste!

Along the way of determining what flavor your Kool-Aid should be, there will be moments, events and situations where you'll wonder if certain ingredients belong in your final mix. This will include different people that are doing nothing more than confusing you and tainting your blend. Remember the old saying: "Too many cooks spoil the broth?"

Don't ever be dissuaded from your chosen path by these 'false gods' you'll run into along the way. As you told me once, 'There are jerks everywhere-you can't get away from them'. Unfortunately, truer words were never spoken. I hope you never lose your keen insight and always realize they're lurking in the bushes nearby.

I think that before **any** person offers advice to someone else, they need to 'have it together'. In fact, in general, I'd tend to be skeptical of anyone who freely offers unsolicited advice, unless it's a loved one or respected family member who has earned your trust and faith as we've already discussed.

It's like the guy who has a commercial on T.V. concerning how he can teach **you** to make a million dollars if you follow **his** investment 'system'. Just send him $29.99 for the video that holds all the secrets and you'll be good to go! Almost without exception, the only person who ever benefits from this arrangement is the guy selling the video. Don't put too much credence in anyone or anything outside of you and your abilities.

I mentioned earlier how you should conduct yourself as though you were being video-taped, 24/7. I want you to be able to hold your head high and be proud of yourself and all that you do, all the time. I want you to be completely satisfied with the person you become.

> *. . . Erin, I'm glad you've taken the time to read this;*
> *let's hope you come up with a terrific, new and*
> *totally fabulous flavor of Kool-Aid all your own!*
> *Love,*
> *Dad*

## DEALING WITH LIFE MUSIC LIST

I am including the titles that are part of my 'Dealing with Life' music list as of December 8, 2008 (my birthday). Listening to this compilation will give the reader an idea of where I'm at in my personal life along with an insight of my beliefs.

Drive-Incubus
Kites Are Fun-Free Design
I Hope You Dance-Lee Ann Womack
Sailing-Christopher Cross
Amazing-Aerosmith
Live Life Like You Are Dying-Tim McGraw
Jesus To A Child-George Michael
Cats In The Cradle-Harry Chapin
Old Man-Neil Young
My Wish-Rascal Flatts
Get Over It-The Eagles
Dirty Laundry-Don Henley
Hard To Say-Dan Fogelberg
Honesty-Billy Joel
Forever In Blue Jeans-Neil Diamond
Don't Worry-Be Happy-Bobby McPherin
Everything Is Different Now-Don Henley
Love Is The Answer-England Dan & John Ford Coley
Another Day-James Taylor
My Father's Eyes-Eric Clapton
Have A Talk With God-Stevie Wonder
Circus-Eric Clapton
Dream On-Aerosmith
New York Minute (Live)-The Eagles
You Gotta Be-Des'ree
Secret O Life-James Taylor
Enough To Be On Your Way-James Taylor

These songs all have a great deal of meaning for me. I believe they can help a person understand what life is about and what to maybe anticipate. A special note: the last song on the list, 'Enough To Be On Your Way' is the song I want played at my memorial service because it truly is enough to be on your way.

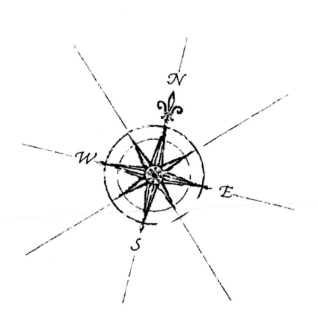

CPSIA information can be obtained at www.ICGtesting.com
Printed in the USA
267235BV00001B/5/P